GW00468329

Private Memoirs of the Duchess of Angoulême Which, With the Work of M. Hue, and the Journal of Cléry, Complete the History of the Captivity of the Royal Family of France in the Temple. Transl., With Notes

by Mary Theresa Charlotte (Duchess of Angoulême.)

Address:
HardPress
8345 NW 66TH ST #2561
MIAMI FL 33166-2626
USA
Email: info@hardpress.net

PRIVATE MEMOIRS,

WHICH,

WITH THE WORK OF M. HUE,

AND

THE JOURNAL OF CLERY,

COMPLETE THE

HISTORY OF THE CAPTIVITY

OF THE

ROYAL FAMILY OF FRANCE

IN THE TEMPLE.

I forgive, from the bottom of my heart, those who have become my persecutors.
(The King's Will.)
I forgive all my enemies the evil which they have done me. *(The Queen's Letter.)*
I beseech you, O my God! to pardon those who have put my parents to death.
(A Prayer, written by Madame Royale on the Walls of her Prison.)

TRANSLATED FROM THE FRENCH,
WITH NOTES BY THE TRANSLATOR.

LONDON:
JOHN MURRAY, ALBEMARLE-STREET.

1817.

Printed by W. CLOWES,
Northumberland-court, Strand, London.

ADVERTISEMENT,

BY

THE TRANSLATOR.

————"Quæque, miserrima vidi
Et quorum pars magna fui"————

THE following pages are written by the only survivor of the Prisoners of the Temple,—the Duchess of Angoulême, Princess Royal of France.

Her name does not indeed appear in the title-page, because, we suppose, it would be contrary to etiquette; but the work is avowed at Paris; and there is hardly a page which does not afford internal evidence of its authenticity.

The notes of which it is composed were either made at the moment by stealth, and with pencils which Her Royal Highness contrived to conceal from her persecutors, or were added immediately after her release from prison.

It will be observed that several passages are obscure, and one or two contradictory: there are frequent repetitions, and a general want of arrangement. All these, which would be defects in a regular history, increase the value of this Journal: they attest its authenticity, and forcibly impress on our minds the cruel circumstances of perplexity and anxiety under which it was written; and the negligence and disorder, if I may use the expression, in which the Princess appears before us, *become* her misery better than a more careful and ornamented attire.

It is a great proof of her good taste, as well as of her conscientious veracity, that she has not permitted any polishing hand to smooth down the colloquial simplicity of her style, and the irregular, but forcible, touches of her expression.

The Translator, on his part, has endeavoured to preserve this characteristic of the original. He might, with greater ease to himself, have adopted a more equal and flowing style; but he felt it to be of more importance to endeavour to give a fac-simile of this curious little work: he has therefore given a version, not always literal, but as close as the idioms of the two languages would admit.

There are some little differences on minor points between Her Royal Highness's account and those of M. Hue and Clery. These might have been easily corrected or omitted: but, again, we think the Duchess has acted with perfect good taste and judgment, in leaving these passages as they were originally written. Those who will take the trouble to compare her's with the two other accounts will see that these trifling variances (and they are very trifling) instead of invalidating, support the credit of all the narrators, and prove that they all faithfully report the impressions or the information which they severally received.

The Translator has added a few notes, which will, he flatters himself, be found useful to those readers who may not be intimately acquainted with the early history of the French Revolution. They are marked T.

T.

NOTE,

BY THE FRENCH EDITOR.

THE Memoirs which we offer to the public cannot fail to excite its curiosity. Every thing that renews the recollection of the virtues of Louis XVI., and every account of his sufferings, have long been received with peculiar interest. A narrative of the persecutions which he underwent excites a painful emotion; and yet, far from seeking to avoid, we take a melancholy pleasure in contemplating the sad picture. Amidst the sufferings of the martyr are mingled the most striking lessons of patience and resignation; and the whole scene commands alike our admiration and our sympathy.

Independently of the general interest which we must feel about these details concerning the royal family, these Memoirs possess the further advantage of serving as a supplement to the works which have already appeared on the subject of the confinement of that family in the Temple. Of these, the journal of Clery, and the work of M. Hue, are alone perfectly genuine; but M. Hue was not a personal witness of the events which took place after the 2d of September, and Clery has not continued his journal beyond the day on which his master perished. From this period no eye-witness has informed us of what passed in the interior of the Temple; and we are left to vague, and often incorrect, reports. It was, of course, highly desirable that this deficiency should be supplied; and it is this object which the Memoirs we now offer to the public completely fulfil.

Many details will, no doubt, be found in them, which have already appeared in the books to which we have alluded; but such repetitions cannot be avoided in relating the same events. There are also several passages which would be rather obscure, if they were not explained by more detailed accounts in the other works; and we must have observed, that we have thought it better to refer generally, for the elucidation of such passages, to the works of M. Hue and Clery, than to explain them by notes copied from those works.

But what reliance, it will be asked, can we place in an account, whose author is unknown? We foresaw this objection; and all that we shall say in reply is, that, if we were permitted to reveal the author's name, we should not have any occasion to recommend the work: it would be felt to be beyond all praise, and its value would have no other measure than that of the attachment of good Frenchmen to the family, a portion of whose sufferings are here described.

We will add, however, that these Memoirs have been committed to writing during the events related, or very shortly afterwards; and that it was, at that moment, little expected they were ever to be published, or that any other eyes than those of a few dear friends should read a simple recital of the unparalleled persecutions of the best of kings, of the most magnanimous of women, and of a child, who, in happier days, would have been, even in his cradle, a pledge of the fortunate destinies of France. It must not, therefore, excite surprise, that negligence of style should be found in these Memoirs: they are evidences of the truth of the narrative, and we have, for that reason, respected them. Publishing—not a *book*, but—mere private *Memoirs*, we should have thought ourselves very blamable if we had attempted to remove the peculiarities of the author's style and manner.

MEMOIRS,

&c. &c.

[1792.]—THE king and his family reached the Temple at seven o'clock in the evening of the 13th August, 1792. The gunners wanted to take him alone to the **Tower*, and to leave the

* The Temple, which had its name, like our Temple, from the knights templars, consisted of two distinct buildings;—the *palace* of the Temple, which faced the Rue du Temple, where one of the princes of the blood usually resided (latterly the Count D'Artois lived there), and the *tower* of the Temple, which was situated in the space behind the palace. The *tower* consisted of a great square tower, with a round tower at each corner; and on one side there was a small addition, which was usually called the Tourelle or Turret, though the small round towers were also so called. The tower of the Temple was so little known in Paris, that some of those who attended the king never saw or heard of it till the

other prisoners in the *Palace* of the Temple, but *Manuel had by the way received an order to conduct the whole family to the *Tower*. Petion appeased the anger of the gunners, and the order was executed. Petion went away, but Manuel remained, and the municipal officers would not let the king out of their sight: he supped with his family. The Dauphin was dying with sleep. At eleven o'clock Madame de Tourzel took him to the tower, which was positively to be the common lodging of all. About one o'clock in the morning, the king

---

fatal night his majesty was confined there. Mr. Hue gives an interesting description of his first and uncertain view of this curious old edifice. Buonaparte, anxious to extinguish all recollections of ancient times, razed the Temple. T.

* We shall give, in the course of the work, notices of the most remarkable personages whose names we may meet; but they occur in such a number in these first pages, that the notes would overwhelm the text. T.

and the rest of the family were conducted thither ;—there was nothing ready for their reception. Madame Elizabeth slept in the kitchen, and it was said that Manuel himself was ashamed at shewing her the way to such a bed-chamber.

These are the names of the persons who were confined with the royal family in this melancholy abode :—

The Princess of Lamballe, Madame de Tourzel, and Pauline her daughter : Messrs. Hue and *Chamilly, who slept in a room above; they belonged to the king : Madame Navarre, waiting-woman to Madame Elizabeth, and who, as well as Pauline, slept in the kitchen with her. Madame St. Brice, who

* First valet-de-chambre of the king. His fidelity to his master affected even the Septembrisers at La Force, who spared his life ; he was, however, brought to the guillotine in June, 1794. T.

took care of the Dauphin; she slept in the billiard-room with him and Madame de Tourzel. Madame Thibaut, the Queen's attendant, and Madame Bazire, Madame Royale's*, lay down stairs. The king had three men, †Turgis, Crétien, and Marchand.

Next day, the 14th, the Dauphin came to breakfast with his mother, and all the family went to visit the great rooms of the Tower, where it was said that accommodations were

---

* The present Duchess of Angoulême, the writer of this journal. *Madame* is the title of the daughters of the kings of France: the eldest is called *Madame Royale*. T.

† These persons had been menial servants of the king, who, with a provident devotion to his person, contrived to get employed in the Temple. Of Crétien and Marchand I know nothing more; but Turgis continued to distinguish himself by his courage and fidelity to the royal family. At the risk of his life he kept up their communication with their friends. Madame Elizabeth peculiarly valued him, and the Duchess of Angoulême has since placed him in her own family. T.

to be prepared for them, as the turret was too small for so many people.

The next day, Manuel and Santerre having come, the prisoners went to walk in the garden. There was great murmuring against the ladies who had followed the royal family: on their arrival they had found some women appointed by Petion to wait upon them; and although they refused to be attended by these women, there was, the next day but one, a decree of the *Commune, directing the departure of those who had come with the royal family; but the king and queen having formally op-

---

* The Commune, or common council of the city o Paris, took very early a prominent share in the revolutionary government. It was often as powerful, and generally more mischievously active, than even the National Assemblies or Convention. All that belonged to the custody, or rather persecution, of the royal family, was, by this atrocious junto, jealously affected to itself. T.

posed this, and the municipal officers who were engaged in the Temple having joined them, the order was for the moment revoked.

All the persons of the royal family passed the day together.—The king taught his son geography; the queen, history, and to get verses by heart; and Madame Elizabeth gave him little lessons in arithmetic. The king had fortunately found a * library, which amused him, and the queen worked tapestry. The municipal officers were very familiar, and shewed little respect even for the king; one of them always kept sight of him. His majesty asked to have a man and woman sent in to do the coarser kind of menial work.

---

* The archives of the Order of Malta were kept in the Tower, and this library was attached to the office of the archivist or keeper. T.

The night between the 19th and 20th August, a new order of the Commune directed the removal from the Temple of all the persons who were not of the royal family. M. Hue and Chamilly were removed from the king, who remained alone with a municipal officer.

They then came down to carry away Madame de Lamballe. The queen strongly opposed this, saying, (what indeed was true,) that this princess was of the royal family * ;

* The princess de Lamballe was of the house of Savoy, and the widow of Louis de Bourbon, Prince de Lamballe, son of the Duke of Penthievre. She was united in the strictest affection and friendship with the queen ; and when the arrangements for the journey to Montmedy, better known by the name of the *flight to Varennes*, obliged them to part for a moment, Madame de Lamballe made her way to England ; but when she heard of the queen's recapture, not all the persuasions of her friends, nor all her own forebodings of her fate, could prevent her hastening to rejoin her royal

—they nevertheless carried her away. Madame Elizabeth went down with Madame de Navarre and Pauline de Tourzel; the municipal officers assured her that these ladies should return when they had been examined. The Dauphin was taken into his mother's apartment, that he might not be left alone. The queen could not tear herself from the arms of Madame de Lamballe. The princesses embraced all these ladies, hoping however to see them next day, and they passed

---

friend; whom she accompanied and cheered, during her dreadful trials, with unexampled fortitude and devotion, till the separation here mentioned; which was followed in a few days by the massacre of this amiable woman, under circumstances of unmanly cruelty and cannibal atrocity, unparalleled in the annals *even of France*. She, as well as the queen, had been the object of the most brutal calumnies: but in the hour of trial, in their agony, and in their death, how nobly did these august persons refute the slanders of their ignorant and malignant libellers! T.

the night without sleep. The king, though awake, also remained in his bed-chamber, and the municipal officers never left him.

Next day, at seven o'clock, their majesties learned that the ladies would not return to the Temple, and that they had been taken to the prison of* La Force: but they were very much surprised, at nine o'clock, to see M. Hue†

* The palace of the noble family of La Force, which had been purchased by the government, and converted into a prison. T.

† M. Hue is the author of a most interesting and valuable work, called " The last Year of the Life and Reign of Louis XVI." This worthy servant has distinguished himself by a fidelity at once chivalrous and useful to his master and his family. He is immortalized in the king's Will. After he was dragged from the Tower, during the massacres of September, 1792, he never forgot his duty; he was still indefatigable in the service of the royal prisoners: there was no sort of danger which he did not risk for them; and his devotion was limited only by his anxiety that they should not lose his services. He accordingly remained in Paris during the whole reign of terror, witnessing the gradual diminution of

return, who said that the council-general of the Commune had pronounced him innocent, and sent him back to the Temple.

After dinner, Petion sent a man of the name of Tison, and his wife, to do the coarse work. The queen took her son into her room, and sent her daughter with Madame Elizabeth. She was only separated from her children by a little room, where a municipal officer and a sentinel were placed. The

---

the royal family by the guillotine, or ill usage; and, in spite of personal danger, never could be persuaded to leave that bloody city till the *Orphan of the Temple* was sent to Germany, when he followed, and rejoined her. He afterwards came with her to England, and was one of those who accompanied Louis XVIII. when he sailed from Dover in April, 1814, to ascend a throne of danger, anxiety, and care; where he needed, almost as much as his unhappy brother, that energy, that self-confidence, that adherence to high principles, that devotion to his friends, that severity towards his enemies, which I lament to think has been wanting to the councils of both. T.

king remained above stairs; but, having learned that they were preparing another apartment for him, which he by no means wished for, because he would be thereby still farther removed from his family, he sent for Palloi *, the foreman of the labourers, to prevent the work being proceeded in; but Palloi replied insolently, that he received no orders but from the Commune.

The princesses and the Dauphin went up every morning to the king's apartment to breakfast; and afterwards the whole family returned to the queen's, where the king passed the day. They went every day to walk in the garden, for the sake of the Dauphin's health, where the king was always

* Palloi's claim to be employed in fortifying the *new* state-prison was his supposed share in the destruction of the *old*. He was a mason, and boasted of being one of the conquerors of the Bastille. T.

insulted by the guard. On the feast of St. Louis, at seven o'clock in the morning, *Ca Ira* was sung under the walls of the Temple.

They learned that morning, by an officer, that *M. de la Fayette had quitted France. Manuel, in a conversation with the king, in the evening, confirmed the report. He brought Madame Elizabeth a letter from her aunts at Rome. It was the last the family received from without. Louis XVI. was no longer called king. He was treated with no kind of respect; and, instead of "Sire," or

* La Fayette, after an alternation of wickedness and weakness, lost all courage and hope; and, abandoning duties which he had arrogated to himself, fled basely enough from a storm of his own raising; leaving the unhappy victims of his follies, his faults, and his perfidy, to perish on the scaffolds of his late associates. His desertion saved him from the guillotine, to be one of Buonaparte's Chamber of Deputies. T.

"Your Majesty," was called only Mr. or Louis. The officers always sat in his presence, and never took off their hats.

They deprived him of his *sword, and they searched his pockets. Petion sent, to wait upon the king, Clery, who had been before in his service; but he, at the same time, sent, as turnkey and gaoler, the horrible man† who had broken open his door on the ‡20th of

---

* See Mr. Hue's touching account of the sensibility with which the king felt this indignity. T.

† The name of this wretch was Rocher: he was a saddler by trade, and afterwards had a commission in the armies. T.

‡ Every body knows that on the 20th of June the king's palace was forced by the mob, in whose hands the royal family remained for several hours. The conduct of all the members of this unhappy family, on this trying occasion, was, in the highest degree, courageous and noble. Two circumstances in particular cannot be too often repeated. At a critical moment of the riot, a grenadier told the king not to be afraid:—the king put the man's hand to his heart, and said, "Feel whether it

June, 1792, and who had been near assassinating him. This man never left the Tower, and was indefatigable in endeavouring to torment him. One time he would sing, before the whole family, the *Carmagnole*, and a thousand other horrors; again, knowing that the queen disliked the smoke of tobacco, he would puff it in her face, as well as in that of the king, as they happened to pass him. He took care always to be in bed before the royal family, because he knew that they must pass through his room to reach theirs. Sometimes, even, he would be in bed as they went to dinner: in short, there was no species of torment or insult that he did not practise. The king suffered it all

---

beats more quickly than usual." The mob, mistaking Madame Elizabeth for the queen, began to ill-treat her: some of the attendants, alarmed for her safety, exclaimed, "It is not the queen!"—"Alas!" said the generous princess, "why do you undeceive them?" T.

with gentleness, forgiving, from the bottom of his heart, these petty persecutions. The queen bore it with a dignity of character that frequently repressed their insolence. The garden was full of workmen, who insulted the king. One of them even boasted before him that he wished to split the queen's head with the tool with which he was working. Petion, however, caused him to be arrested.

These insults were redoubled on the 2d of September. They even threw stones in at the king's window, which fortunately did not touch him; but, about the same time, a woman, probably with good intentions, wrote on a large piece of paste-board, "*Verdun is taken,*" and held it up to a window*. Madame Elizabeth had time to

---

* The windows of the houses in the adjoining streets overlooked the garden of the Temple. T.

read it, though none of the officers saw it. Hardly had the king heard this news, when a new municipal officer, named Mathieu *, arrived; he was in a furious passion, and ordered the king to go in: all the family followed, fearing to be separated from his majesty.

On going up stairs, Mathieu found Mr. Hue, whom he seized by the collar, crying out, that he arrested him. Mr. Hue, to gain time to receive the commands of their majesties, asked for some delay, that he might pack up his effects. Mathieu refused; but another officer, less brutal, consented. Mathieu then turned to the king, and said to him every thing that the most

* Almost the last words Louis spoke were to ask pardon of this wretch, whose brutality had betrayed the king into an expression of impatience. Clery calls him Mathey; but it was the same person. T.

brutal rage could suggest: amongst the rest he exclaimed—"The drum has beat to arms; the tocsin has sounded; the alarm-guns have been fired; the emigrants are at Verdun; if they come we shall all perish, but *you shall die first!*"

The king heard all this, and a thousand such sallies, with the calm that hope inspires. The Dauphin burst out crying, and ran into another room. Madame Royale followed him, and had the greatest difficulty in quieting him. Mr. Hue now came back, and, after Mathieu had gone through his violence over again, they went away together. Fortunately, Mr. Hue was taken only to the Town-House, for the massacre was already begun at the Abbaye. He remained a month in prison; but, when he was released, he did not return to the Temple.

The other officers all disapproved the ferocious conduct of Mathieu, but they could do no more. They told the king that it was universally believed that the king of Prussia was advancing and killing all the French he met, under an order signed *Louis*. There was no species of calumny which they did not invent, even the most ridiculous and impossible. The queen, who could not sleep, heard the drums beating all night, but, in the Tower, it was not known why.

The 3d of September, Manuel* came to

---

* An attorney, son of a porter, tutor in a gentleman's family, and at last a Jacobin and Conventionalist. He was the attorney-general of the commune of Paris, the soul of the insurrection of the 20th of June, and a great contributor to that of the 10th of August. He moved that the king should be sent to the Temple, volunteered to be his gaoler there, and became his proselyte. Touched by the candour, virtue, and innocence, of the royal family, "almost he was persuaded to become" a royalist. He

assure the king that Madame de Lamballe, and all the other persons who had been removed from the Temple, were well, and in security together, in the prison of La Force. At three o'clock, just after dinner, and as the king was sitting down to tric-trac with the queen (which he played for the purpose of having an opportunity of saying a few words to her unheard by the keepers), the most horrid shouts were heard. The officer who happened to be on guard in the room behaved well: he shut the door and the window, and even drew the curtains, to prevent

---

voted against the king's death, he denounced the massacres, and, after escaping assassination, perished on the scaffold, the 14th of November, 1793, at the age of forty-two. The dreadful moment, to him, must have been when, on his reaching his prison, his fellow-sufferers assailed him with every mark of indignation, for crimes which he had now learned to detest as much as they did. T.

their seeing any thing; but, on the outside, the workmen, and the gaoler, Rocher, joined the assassins, and increased the tumult.

Several officers of the guard and of the municipality now arrived: the former insisted that the king should shew himelf at the windows; fortunately the latter opposed it; but, on his majesty's asking what was the matter, a young officer of the guard replied, "Well! since you will know, it is the head of Madame de Lamballe that they want to shew you." At these words the queen was overcome with horror; it was the only occasion in which her firmness abandoned her. The municipal officers were very angry with this young man; but the king, with his usual goodness, excused him, saying, that it was not the officer's fault, but his own, since he had questioned him.

The noise lasted till five o'clock. The

prisoners learned that the people had wished to force the door, and that the municipal officers had been enabled to prevent it only by putting a tri-coloured scarf across it, and by allowing six of the murderers to march round the tower with the head of the princess, leaving at the door her body, which they would have dragged in also. When this deputation entered, Rocher shouted for joy, and brutally insulted a young man who turned sick with horror at this spectacle.

It was hardly over, when Petion*, instead

---

* Petion, an advocate of Chartres, a tool of the Duke of Orleans, member of the States-General, mayor of Paris, a conventionalist, and a regicide. He and Robespierre were called *two fingers of the same hand*; but he soon found, that Robespierre had four fingers against his one. Their enmity was almost as bloody as their friendship had been. Petion was outlawed; and, escaping the gentler death of the scaffold, was found in the woods dead, and half-devoured by wild beasts. T.

of exerting himself to stop the massacres, coolly sent his secretary to the king with some money. This man was very ridiculous, and said a thousand things which at another moment would have made one laugh. He thought the queen was standing up out of respect for him; because, since this dreadful scene, she had remained standing and motionless, perfectly insensible of all that was going on. The municipal officer, who had given his scarf to tie across the door, took care to make Clery* pay him the value.

---

* Clery, the author of a most interesting "Journal of "what passed in the Tower of the Temple, during the "Captivity of Louis XVI." Of a lower rank, and possessing less power of being useful, Clery's affectionate and heroic fidelity places him nevertheless by the side of Monsieur Hue. Clery did not live to see the restoration; he died at Vienna on the 10th of June, 1809; and on his tomb is inscribed, "Here lies the faithful Clery!" T.

The drum continued to beat to arms all night, and the two princesses, who could not sleep, listened to the sobs of the queen, which never ceased. It was believed in the Tower that the massacre had ceased on the first day, and it was only some time after that they learned that it had lasted three.

It is impossible to describe all the violent sçenes which were occasioned, as well by the municipal officers as by the guard; every thing alarmed their guilty consciences. One day, a man having fired a gun in the Temple, to try it, they examined him with great ceremony, and drew up a formal account of the transaction. Another time, during supper, there was a cry "To arms!"—they believed the Prussians were coming. The brutal Rocher drew his sabre, and said to the king, " *If they come, I shall*

" *kill you.*" It was nothing, however, but some mistake of the patroles.

On one occasion, however, about a hundred tradesmen, led by some friend of the royal family, undertook to force the gate at the side of the *Rotunda; the guard and municipal officers hurried to the spot; the tradesmen were dispersed, and perhaps, alas! there were some lives lost.

The severity of these municipal officers increased daily. There were, however, two of them who alleviated the sufferings of the august prisoners, by shewing them pity, and by giving them hopes. There was also one sentinel, who, through the key-hole, had a conversation with Madame Elizabeth. This

---

* A circular building on the N.E. side of the enclosure of the Temple. T.

poor man did nothing but weep the whole time he was in the Temple; may Heaven have rewarded him for his affectionate attachment to the king!

Madame Royale was employed in ciphering, and the queen wrote out extracts of books for her; but a municipal officer continually looked over their shoulders, so great was their fear of conspiracies. They had refused the newspapers to the prisoners, that they might not know the state of affairs abroad. One day, however, they brought one to the king, telling him it contained something interesting for him. Monsters!—the king found that an artillery-man demanded "the head of the tyrant, that he might load his piece with it, and fire it against the enemy!" The calm and contemptuous silence of the king disappointed the malice of those who had sent this infernal writing. There was also a municipal officer who came one night, and, after a thousand insults, repeated what had been before said, that, if the enemy advanced, the whole royal family should perish. "The child, indeed," he said, "excited some pity; but that, being the son of a tyrant, he must needs die with the rest." These were the scenes which each day brought with it.

The republic was proclaimed on the 22d September; they communicated it with great joy to the prisoners: this day they also reported the retreat of the Prussians.

In the beginning of October they removed pens, paper, ink, and pencils; they searched every where, even with rudeness: the queen, however, and Madame Elizabeth, concealed some pencils, which they preserved.

The evening of the same day, after the king

had supped, he was told to stop, that he was not to return to his former apartments, and that he was to be separated from his family. At this dreadful sentence the queen lost her usual courage: the princesses quitted the king with abundance of tears, though they expected to see him again in the morning.

In the morning, however, they brought them their breakfast separately; the queen would take nothing. The officers, alarmed at her silent and concentrated sorrow, allowed the *princesses to see the king, but at meal-times only, and on condition that they should not speak low, nor in any foreign language, but loud, and in *good French*. They went down therefore with the greatest joy, to dine with

* Here, and in most other places, until their final separation, the queen is included under the term *Princesses*. T.

the king. One of the officers observed that Madame Elizabeth had spoken low to the king: he chid her violently.

At supper, when the Dauphin was in bed, the queen and Madame Elizabeth sat with him alternately, while the other went with Madame Royale to sup with the king. In the mornings, after breakfast, the princesses remained in the king's apartments, while Clery dressed their hair, as he was no longer allowed to come to the queen's room, and they had, besides, by this arrangement, the pleasure of spending a few moments more with the king.

One day Manuel came to his majesty, and took from him, with great rudeness, his *red

* The Cordon of St. Louis. The Order of the St. Esprit had been abolished by the assembly; and the king, scrupulous in obeying even the most unjust decrees which took the shape of a law, ceased to wear it. T.

ribbon. He assured him, that, of all the persons who had been in the Temple, Madame de Lamballe alone had perished. They made Clery, Tison, and his wife, take an oath of fidelity to *the nation*.

One night a municipal officer awakened the Dauphin suddenly, that he might see that he was safe; this was the only occasion in which the queen shewed any impatience at the conduct of these people. One of them told the queen that Petion's design was not the death of the king, but to confine him for life with his son, in the castle of Chambord. I cannot tell what this man's object could be in repeating this story, for he never came again.

They had now placed the king in an apartment under that of the queen: the Dauphin slept in the latter. Clery and a municipal officer slept in the king's apartments. The windows were blocked up with new gratings and blinds; the chimneys were only stove-funnels, and smoked very much.

The following is the way the prisoners passed their days.

The king arose at seven, and was employed in his devotions till eight. Afterwards he dressed himself and his son, and at nine came to breakfast with the queen. After breakfast the king taught the Dauphin his lessons till eleven. The child then played till twelve, at which hour the whole family was obliged to walk in the garden*, whatever the weather might be; because the guard, which was relieved at that time, wished to see all the prisoners, and

* This, it will be seen, applies only to a small portion of the time. The luxury of a walk in the garden was soon denied to them. T.

satisfy themselves that they were safe. The walk lasted till dinner, which was at two o'clock. After dinner their majesties played at tric-trac or piquet, that they might have an opportunity of saying a few words to one another. At four o'clock, the queen, her sister, and children, generally retired, as the king was accustomed to sleep a little at this hour. At six the Dauphin went down again to his father to say his lessons, and to play till supper-time. After supper, at nine o'clock, the queen undressed him quietly, and put him to bed. The princesses then went up to their own apartment again, and the king did not go to bed till eleven. The queen worked a good deal of tapestry: she directed the studies of Madame Royale, and often made her read aloud to her. Madame Elizabeth was frequently in prayer, and read every morning the divine service of the day. She read a good deal in books of piety, and sometimes, at the queen's request, would read aloud to them.

The municipal officers brought the newspapers to the royal family, that they might see the retreat of the Prussians, and the horrid libels against the king, of which they were full. One day, some of these people said to the princesses, " Come, ladies, I have good news for you; several emigrant traitors have been taken: if you are patriots, you must be glad of it." The queen, as usual, made no reply, and did not even appear to hear them. Her calm contempt, and her dignified air, generally struck them with respect. They seldom ventured to speak to *her*.

A *deputation of the Convention came, for the first time, to see the king in the Temple: the members asked him whether he had not any complaint to make. He replied No; that, provided he was permitted to remain with his family, he was happy. Clery complained that the tradesmen who supplied the Temple were not paid. Chabot answered, "The nation is not reduced to half-a-crown." These deputies were Chabot†, Dupont‡,

* The names of the members of this deputation, as given by Clery, differ a little from Madame's—neither, perhaps, mention *all* that came. T.

† Chabot, a capuchin, an apostate and a regicide: he was guillotined on the 5th of April, 1794. T.

‡ Dupont, one of those cold-blooded philosophers who affected to discuss abstract questions, while their colleagues were shedding the noblest blood of Europe. He was a regicide, and boasted in the tribune that he was an atheist: these two qualities could not fail to recommend him to Buonaparte, who employed him. T.

Drouet*, and Le Cointre-Puyravaux†: they came again after dinner, to repeat the same questions. One day Drouet came alone, and asked the queen if she had no complaint to make. She made him no answer.

A short time after, as they were at dinner,

* Drouet, the famous post-master of St. Menehoud, who arrested the king at Varennes, had been a dragoon; but, by this event, was dragged into notice, and elected to the Convention; amongst the ignorant and brutal members of which, he was remarkable for his ignorance and brutality. He was one of Buonaparte's *sous-prefets* during his first reign, and one of his Chamber of Representatives in the second. He was worthy all the distinction which Napoleon could confer on him, and of the mingled ridicule and execration of the rest of mankind. T.

† Le Cointre-Puyravaux, a lawyer and regicide. He pronounced his judgment in the following elegant and logical formula:—"I represent the people; the people has been assassinated by the tyrant. I vote for the death of the tyrant." So late as 1798, he wished to enforce the atrocious sentence of death against the emigrants. He was one of Buonaparte's commissaries of police in his reign of 1815, but I know not what has since become of him. T.

some gendarmes arrived, who fell upon Clery, and forced him off to one of the tribunals. Some days before, Clery, in going down stairs in company with one of the municipal officers, had met a young man of his acquaintance, who was on guard. They wished one another good morning, and shook hands. The officers took umbrage at this, and caused the young man to be arrested. It was to be confronted with him before the tribunal that Clery was now taken. The king entreated he might be allowed to return. The municipal officers said he would not return. He did, however, return.

One day a great noise was heard of a mob crying out for the heads of Louis and Marie Antoinette. They had the cruelty to yell these demands under the windows of the prisoners.

The king was ill of a violent cold. They permitted him to send for a physician and an apothecary, Lemonnier and Robert. The Commune was uneasy; there was a regular bulletin of his health. He got better. The whole family had colds, but the king's was the most serious.

The Commune was changed the 2d of December. The newly-elected municipal officers came at ten o'clock at night to **reconnoitre* the royal family. Some days after, there was a decree of this new Commune, to turn away Clery and Tison; to take from the prisoners their knives, scissors, and other sharp instruments; and, finally, that whatever they ate

---

* This will seem a strange expression, but it is the very word used by the duchess, and I know not how I could better xpress the hostile and prying visits of thece men. T.

should be previously and carefully tasted. A search was made for sharp instruments: the princesses gave up their scissors.

On the 11th of December, the sound of a drum, and the noise of the arrival of troops at the Temple, gave the prisoners some uneasiness. The king came down with the young prince after breakfast. At eleven o'clock, Chambon*

* A physician of little note, raised to the infamous dignity of mayor of Paris, by the almost incredible accident of having opponents baser and more obscure than himself. He was an Orleanist, and partook the character of his party, for he was as weak as he was wicked. He was despised by all parties, and chiefly by his own, which knew him best. His life ended as it began, in obscurity. I have not been able to discover when he died.

He must not be confounded with Chambon, the conventionalist, who voted for the death of the king, but with an appeal to the people; and who was killed in a farm at Lubersac, in 1793, in the overthrow of the Orleanist party, to which he also belonged. T.

and Chaumette*, the mayor and attorney-general of the Commune, and Colombeau †, the secretary, arrived. They announced to the king a decree of the Convention, that his majesty should be brought to its bar to be examined. They obliged him to send the Dauphin to his mother's apartment; but, not having the decree of the Convention, they

* Attorney of the Commune of Paris, son of a shoemaker; he was successively a cabin-boy, a postilion, a stationer's clerk, and an attorney. He was for a long while the idol of the mob, and the terror and scourge of Paris; but at last even Robespierre felt alarmed at his audacious profaneness and cruelty, and he enveloped him in the proscription of the Hebertists. There is a striking description of the meanness and cowardice of this wretch, when he met in prison crowds that he had himself sent thither. He was guillotined on the 13th April, 1794; and the only truth he ever, perhaps, spoke, were his last words, "That those who had sent him there deserved to follow him." T.

† I know nothing of Colombeau, but that he was one of the municipality of the 10th of August. This office, and the anecdote in the text, sufficiently characterize him.

kept the king waiting two hours. He did not go till about one o'clock, when he went in the mayor's carriage with Chaumette and Colombeau. The carriage was escorted by municipal officers on foot. The king observing, as they went along, that Colombeau saluted a great number of persons, asked him if they were all friends of his; Colombeau answered, "They are brave citizens of the 10th of August, whom I never see but with the greatest pleasure."

I shall not say any thing of the conduct of the king at the bar of the Convention. All the world knows it: his firmness, his mildness, his goodness, his courage, in the midst of an assembly of cannibals thirsting for his blood, can never be forgotten, and must be admired by the latest posterity.

The king returned at six o'clock to the

tower of the Temple, under the same escort. It is impossible to describe the anxiety which his family had suffered in his absence. The queen had used every endeavour with the officers who guarded her, to discover what was passing; it was the first time she had condescended to question them. These men would tell her nothing. It was only on the king's arrival that she was informed.

When he returned, she asked to see him instantly. She made the same request to Chambon, but received no answer. The Dauphin passed the night with her; and, as he had no bed, she gave him hers, and sat up all night in the deepest distraction. The other princesses were afraid to leave her in so melancholy a state; but she obliged them to go to bed.

Next day, she again asked to see the

king, and to read the newspapers, that she might learn the course of the trial. She entreated, that at least, if she was to be denied this indulgence, his children might see him. This request was referred to the Commune. The newspapers were refused; but the children were allowed to see their father on condition of being *entirely separated* from their mother. When this was conveyed to the king, he said that the important business which then occupied him would not allow of his attending altogether to his son, and that his daughter should not quit her mother. The Dauphin's bed was in consequence removed into the queen's room.

The Convention came to see the king. He asked for *counsel, ink, paper, and razors.

* It ought never to be forgotten that Louis had the noble confidence to select for his counsel, against a

All these requests were granted. Messrs. * Malesherbes, † Tronchet, and Desèze, who were assigned as his counsel, came to see him. He was often obliged, in order to converse with them without being overheard, to retire into the turret.

---

charge of violating the constitution, one of the chief framers of that constitution, the lawyer Target; and that this wretched preacher of law and liberty, and liberality, had the baseness to decline this honourable, and, to a man of professional feeling, indispensable duty. T.

* M. de Malesherbes was illustrious by his life, and even, if possible, more so by his death, which was as heroic as that of Sir Thomas More. He was the relation of M. de Chateaubriand, whom his majesty, Louis XVIII., admitted into his council at Ghent, and expelled from it at Paris. M. de Chateaubriand's fate, and his majesty's feelings, are, in this instance, the converse of those of their predecessors, for Louis XVI., who had dismissed Malesherbes from the ministry in his happier days, recalled him to his assistance in the hour of adversity. T.

† Tronchet a little impaired the character he had obtained by his accepting the defence of the king, by taking an office under the usurper. He died in March, 1810. T.

He went no more into the garden, nor did the princesses. He knew nothing of them, as they knew nothing of him, but through the municipal officers. The young princess had something the matter with her foot; and her father, having heard of it, was, with his usual tenderness, very uneasy about her, and made constant inquiries. The family were so fortunate as to find, amongst the members of the Commune, some men, whose compassion alleviated their sufferings. They assured the queen that the king would not be put to death, and that his case would be referred to the primary assemblies, who would undoubtedly save him.

Alas! they deceived themselves; or, through pity, intended to deceive.

On the 26th December, * St. Stephen's

* Some expectation seems to have been entertained,

day, the king made his will, because he expected to be assassinated that day on his way to the bar of the Convention. He went thither, nevertheless, with his usual calmness, and left to *M. Desèze the care of his defence. He left the Temple at eleven o'clock, and returned at three. Henceforward he saw his counsel every day.

[1793.]—At last, on the 18th January, the day on which the sentence was pronounced, the municipal officers entered the king's room at eleven o'clock, saying, that they had now

---

that the feast of the proto-martyr was to be further stained by the martyrdom of the eldest son of the church: a title of which the kings of France were proud. T.

* M. Desèze has been consistent in the course of integrity and honour. He is now first president of the high court of appeals, in France. We are surprised that the present ministry (Feb. 1817) tolerate such an *ultra-royalist* as a man who even ventured his life in the king's defence. T.

orders never to lose sight of him for a moment. He asked if his fate was decided. They answered, No.

Next morning M. Malesherbes came to acquaint him that the sentence had been pronounced; "but, Sire," he added, "these wretches are not yet masters, and every honest man will endeavour to save his master, or will die at his feet." "M. de Malesherbes," said the king, "such proceedings would involve a great many persons, and would excite a civil war in Paris.—*I had rather die.*—You will therefore, I entreat of you, command them from me, to make no effort to save me—the King of France never dies!"

After this conference he was never allowed to see his counsel again. He addressed a note to the municipal officers, to ask to see them, and to complain of the hardship of being kept under perpetual inspection. No attention was paid to his representations.

On Sunday, the 20th January, * Garat, the minister of justice, and the other members of the executive power, came to announce to him the sentence for his execution next day. The king heard it with fortitude and piety: he demanded a respite of three days, to know what the fate of his family was to be, and to have a catholic confessor. The respite was refused. Garat assured him that there was no charge against his family, and that it would be sent

* Garat, an editor of a newspaper, and minister of *justice!*—the friend of Pâche and Hebert, the tool and almost the victim of Robespierre. He survived, however, and became one of the vilest adulators of Buonaparte, who made this jacobin a count of the empire; this sans-culotte, a knight of the legion of honour; this man of the 10th of August, a legislator; in which character he shewed his gratitude, by voting, in March, 1814, for deposing Napoleon the First; and in 1815 he was again for deposing him, but it was only to put in his place Napoleon the Second. I know not what is become of him. T.

out of France. M.* Edgeworth de Firmont was the priest he wished for. He gave his address, and Garat brought him. The king dined as usual, which surprised the municipal officers, who expected that he would endeavour to commit suicide.

The rest of the family learned the sentence by the newsmen, who came about seven o'clock in the evening, crying it under their windows.

A decree of the Convention permitted them to see the king. They ran to his apartment; they found him much altered; he wept for them, and not for fear of death; he related his

* Henry Essex Edgeworth was born at Edgeworth's-town, in Ireland, of which his father was vicar; but he resigned this preferment on account of religious scruples, and removed with his family into France, where they embraced the Roman-Catholic faith. The name of Firmont was derived from Firmount, a family estate in the county of Longford. They were near relations of Mr. Edgeworth, who, as well as his daughter, are so well known in the literary world. T.

trial to the queen, apologizing for the wretches who had condemned him; he told her, that it was proposed to attempt to save him by having recourse to the primary assemblies, but that he would not consent, lest it should excite confusion in the country. He then gave his son some religious advice, and, above all, to forgive those who caused his death; and he gave him his blessing, as well as to his sister.

The queen was very desirous that the whole family should pass the night with the king; but he opposed this, observing to her how much he needed some hours of repose and quiet. She asked at least to be allowed to see him next morning, to which he consented. But, when they were gone, he requested that they might not be permitted to come, as it afflicted him too much. He then remained with his confessor till midnight, when he went to bed.

He slept till he was awakened by the drums at five o'clock. At six, the Abbé Edgeworth said mass, and administered the holy sacrament to the king. At nine o'clock he left the Temple. On the stairs, he delivered his Will to a municipal officer, and a sum of money, which M. de Malesherbes had brought him, and which he desired should be returned to him; but the officers shared it amongst themselves. He met one of the * turnkeys, whom he had reprimanded rather sharply the day before: he now said to him, " *Mathieu, I am sorry for* " *having offended you.*" On his way to the scaffold, he read the prayers for those at the point of death.

On the scaffold he wished to have spoken to the people; but † Santerre prevented him

* The atrocious Mathieu, before mentioned. T.

† A brewer in the Fauxbourg St. Antoine, the most po-

by ordering the drums to beat: what he said was heard by very few. He then undressed himself without assistance. His hands were tied, not with a rope, but with his own handkerchief. At the instant of death, his con-

---

pulous and turbulent part of Paris. His weight in that quarter, and his violent character, advanced him to the chief command of the National Guard of Paris; a distinction which his natural ferocity justified. Though he had no kind of military talents, he had great pretensions, and actually marched at the head of a considerable army, to effect the conquest of La Vendée, according to plans of his own devising. He was beaten every where. One time he was missing, and it was thought that he had been killed in the field of battle; a death so much too honourable for him, that the following derisory epitaph was circulated on the occasion:—

"Ci git le Général Santerre,
"Qui n'eut de Mars que la *bière*."

In confirmation of the old proverb, he and Robespierre soon disagreed, and the death of the latter only saved the former, who afterwards lived quietly in Paris, having contrived to remunerate himself for his public services by obtaining a grant of the vast space on which the Temple stood. T.

fessor exclaimed, "Son of St. Louis, ascend "to heaven *!"

He received the stroke † of death on the Sunday, the 21st of January, 1793, at ten minutes past ten o'clock in the forenoon.

Thus died Louis XVI., king of France, at the age of thirty-nine years, five months, and three days, of which he had reigned eighteen. He had been five months and eight days in prison.

Such are the most remarkable events of his rigorous captivity. During it, he displayed the highest piety, greatness of mind, and good-

* This sublime exclamation was so much the impulse of the Abbé's feelings at the moment, that he had uttered it unconsciously. Indeed, he said afterwards, that he was nearly unconscious of all that passed at that dreadful crisis.—See his Memoirs, by C. S. Edgeworth, London, 1815. T.

† The reader will not fail to observe, that the name of the fatal instrument which deprived her parents of existence is never once mentioned by Madame. T.

ness;—mildness, fortitude, and patience, in bearing the most infamous insults, the most horrid and malignant calumnies;—Christian clemency, which forgave even his murderers; and the love of God, his family, and his people, of which he gave the most affecting proofs, even with his last breath, and of which he went to receive the reward in the bosom of his almighty and all-merciful Creator.

On the morning of this terrible day, the princesses rose at six. The night before, the queen had scarcely strength enough to put her son to bed. She threw herself, dressed as she was, upon her own bed, *where she was heard shivering with cold and grief all night long*. At a quarter past six, the door opened: the princesses believed that they were sent for to see the king; but it was only the officers looking for a prayer-book for the king's mass.

They did not, however, abandon the hope of seeing him, till the shouts of joy of the infuriated populace came to tell them that all was over!

In the afternoon, the queen asked leave to see Clery, who had remained with the king till his last moments*, and who had probably some message for her. The two other princesses were anxious that she should receive this shock of seeing Clery, in hopes of its occasioning a burst of grief, which might relieve her from that state of silent and choaking agony in which they saw her.

In fact, Clery had been intrusted by his master with delivering to the queen her wedding-ring †, with a message that he never would

* Clery was not permitted to accompany the king beyond the Temple, so that this expression means *till his departure from the prison*. T.

† This was, I presume, a ring given to the king by the queen, on their marriage. In the Moniteur of the 25th of January, 1793, it is described as a gold ring, with the

have parted with it but with his life. He had also given him a parcel with the hair of all his family, saying, that it had been so dear to him, that he had carefully preserved it till that moment. The officers reported that Clery was in a frightful state, and in despair, at not being allowed to see the princesses. The queen made her request to the commissioners of the Commune; she also demanded mourning for her family. Clery was kept for a month longer in the Temple, and then released.

The princesses had now a little more freedom; the guards even believed that they were about to be sent out of France; but nothing could calm the agony of the queen. No

---

following inscription engraved on the inside: "M. A. A. A. 19 Aprille, 1770; meaning, I suppose, Marie Antoinette, Archiduchesse d'Autriche. The marriage took place the 16th of May, 1770. T.

hope could touch her heart; because life was indifferent to her, and she did not fear death. She would sometimes look upon her children and her sister with an air of pity which made them shudder. *Fortunately** the affliction of the young princess increased her illness to so serious a degree, that it made a diversion in the mind of her mother, and her despair gave way to maternal alarm. The physician Brunier, and the surgeon Lacase, were sent for. They cured her in the course of a month. The princesses were allowed to see the persons who brought their mourning, but only in presence of the municipal officers.

The queen would go no more to the garden, because she must have passed the door of the room the king had inhabited, and that she could not bear; but, fearing lest want of air should prove injurious to her son and daugh-

* What a touching expression of extreme grief! T.

ter, she asked, about the end of February, to be permitted to walk upon the leads, which was granted.

It was discovered, in the room of the municipal officers, that the sealed parcel which contained the seal, the ring, and some other things of the king's, had been broken open, and the things carried away. These men were very uneasy about this for a short time, but at last they believed that the things had been taken by some thief, for the sake of the gold in which the trinkets were set. But the person who took them was no thief; he acted with the best intentions, to save them for the queen, who desired that the ring and seal should be carefully preserved for her son. I know who this worthy man was; but, alas! he has since died for another good action.

When Dumouriez left France, the prisoners were again more closely confined. A wall was built between the tower and the garden. A kind of blind was erected on the parapet of the leads, and every hole stopped up with the greatest care.

On the 25th of March, the chimney took fire. It was that evening that Chaumette, attorney of the Commune, came, for the first time, to *reconnoitre* the queen, and to know whether she wanted any thing. She asked nothing but a door of communication with her sister's room. The officers opposed this; but Chaumette said, that, in the state of decline in which the queen's health appeared, this indulgence might be necessary, and that he would speak of it to the general council of the Commune. Next morning he returned, at ten o'clock, with * Pâche the mayor, and

* The son of the Mareschal de Castries' porter. This nobleman had given him some education. He was elected mayor on the 15th February, 1793. But, though a

that dreadful Santerre, the commander-in-chief of the national guard. Chaumette told the queen that he had mentioned her request for the door to the council, but that it had been rejected. Pâche asked her whether she had no complaint to make. She, without attending to what he was saying, answered "No" mechanically.

A short time after this, some officers happened to be on guard, whose compassion alleviated in some degree the sorrows of the prisoners. They latterly had attained a great facility in distinguishing the sentiments of the people who came to watch them; the queen particularly, who often prevented the other princesses from being the dupes of false pretences of pity.

---

furious Jacobin, Robespierre wished to get rid of him, and he escaped the scaffold, which he deserved, only by Robespierre's fall. He has since lived in obscurity.

But persecutions of all sorts increased. Tison was prohibited from seeing his daughter; this vexed him. One évening, seeing a stranger admitted, who brought some clothes to Madame Elizabeth, he flew into a rage that this man should be admitted while his friends were excluded. He let fall some expressions which were reported to Pâche, who happened to be down stairs, and who immediately determined to examine Tison. He asked him what had dissatisfied him. He replied, "The not seeing my daughter; and the seeing certain other persons here, who do not conduct themselves as they ought. Certain of the municipal officers have spoken low to the queen and Madame Elizabeth." He was asked their names: he stated them, and added, that the princesses had correspondences without.—When asked for his proofs, he replied, "That one evening, at supper, the queen, in pulling out her pocket-handkerchief, had dropped a pencil; and that one day he had found some wafers and a pen in a box in Madame Elizabeth's room." After this deposition, which he signed, his wife was examined. She repeated the same story; accused several of the officers; asserted that the princesses had had communication with the king during his trial; and denouncéd Brunier, the physician, who attended the younger Madame for her sore foot, as having brought them intelligence. She also, induced by her husband, signed all this; but she bitterly repented it, as we shall see hereafter. This denunciation was made on the 19th of April. She saw her daughter next day.

On the 20th, at half past ten o'clock, the queen and her daughter had just gone to bed, when Hebert* arrived, with several municipals.

* The editor of the most infamous of the revolutionary

They got up hastily; and these men read them a decree of the Commune, which directed that they should be * searched without reserve; this decree was accurately obeyed, even to searching their beds. The Dauphin was asleep: they tore him from his bed, under pretence of searching it. His mother took him up shivering with cold. All they found were a shopkeeper's address, which they took from the queen; a stick of sealing-wax from Madame Elizabeth; and,

---

newspapers, the *Journal du Père Duchême.* It was by the express orders of this monster that Madame de Lamballe was massacred. After having sent numbers of his own associates to the scaffold, he was, at last, sent thither himself, on the 21st of March, 1794. He had married a nun, who was guillotined a few days after him.

* "De les fouiller à discrétion." This phrase is, thank Heaven! untranslatable into our language: none but the monsters of the French age of liberality and reason could have thought *à fouiller à discrétion des femmes.* T.

from the young Madame, *a heart dedicated to our Saviour, and a prayer for the happiness of France. This search lasted till four o'clock in the morning. They made a formal inventory of all they found, which they obliged the queen and Madame Elizabeth to sign, by threatening that, if they did not do so, they should be separated from the royal children. They were exasperated at finding only such trifles.

Three days after they came again, and then sent for Madame Elizabeth alone.

They examined her on the subject of a hat which they had found in her room. They asked her where she got it, how long she had had it, and why she kept it. She answered, that it had belonged to the king, that he had worn it during the first days of his residence

* Religious trinkets of this kind are hung round the necks of children in Roman-Catholic countries. T.

in the Temple, and that she had asked it of him as a keep-sake. The municipal officers replied, that this hat was a suspicious circumstance; and, although she insisted on keeping it, they took it from her, and obliged her to sign her answer.

The queen went every day on the leads, for the sake of giving air to the children. The Dauphin had for some days complained of a stitch in his side; but on the 9th of May, at seven in the evening, he was seized with a violent fever, accompanied with head-ach, and still the pain in his side. During the first days he would not lie in bed, for he complained that he was suffocating. His mother was alarmed, and asked the officers to send for a physician. They assured her that the illness was nothing, and that her maternal anxiety had alarmed her without cause: they, however, mentioned it to the council, and asked, in the queen's name, for Brunier. The council refused to hear of the Dauphin's illness, because Hebert reported that he had seen him at five o'clock, and that he had then no fever. They therefore positively refused the attendance of Brunier, the same, it will be recollected, whom Tison had lately denounced.

The fever, however, grew worse and worse, and Madame Elizabeth came to take Madame Royale's place in the queen's room, in order that this young person might not be exposed to the infectious air of the disease, and that she might assist her sister in attending on the sick boy.

The young princess slept then in her aunt's room. The fever lasted several days, and was always most violent towards evening.

The queen continued every day to request the attendance of a physician, but could not obtain it. At last, on Sunday morning, Thierry came; he was physician of the prisons, and appointed by the Commune to attend the Dauphin. As he came in the morning, he did not perceive much fever; but the queen having requested him to call again in the afternoon, he found it violent, and he undeceived the municipal officers as to their opinion that the queen was alarmed at a trifle. He said, on the contrary, that it was more serious than she believed. He had, at the same time, the civility to call upon Brunier, to consult with him on the case, and as to the medicines which it might be proper to give him, because Brunier was acquainted with the Dauphin's constitution, having attended him from his infancy. He gave him some which did him good; on Wednesday he made him take physic, and that night the young princess came to sleep in her mother's room, who was alarmed about the effect of the Dauphin's medicine, because, the last time he had taken any, he had had dreadful convulsions. She feared lest he might have them again. She never closed her eyes all night: the Dauphin, however, took his physic quietly, and it did him good, and occasioned no trouble.

Some days after, he took a second medicine, which also seemed to agree with him, except that he felt incommoded with heat. He had fits of fever, but only now and then, and occasionally the pain in the side. But his health began to decline, and was never re-established: want of air and exercise did him great mischief, as well as the kind of life which this poor child led, who, at eight years old, passed his days amidst the tears and terrors of his friends, and in constant anxiety and agony.

On the 31st of May, the princesses heard the drum beat to arms, and the tocsin ring, without being able to learn what the noise was about. They were forbidden to go on the leads to take the air,—a prohibition which was always renewed when there was any commotion in Paris.

In the beginning of June, Chaumette and Hebert came one evening about six o'clock, and inquired once more of the queen whether she wanted any thing, or had any thing to complain of. She answered, No. But Madame Elizabeth asked for the * hat which has been already spoken of, and which he (Chaumette) had taken away from her. He

* See page 62. T.

replied, the council had not thought proper to restore it. Then Madame Elizabeth, seeing that Chaumette did not go away, and knowing how extremely her sister suffered (though she gave no sign of it) from his presence, she asked him why he came, and if he was to stay. Chaumette answered, that being on a visit to the prisons, and all prisons being equal, he had come to the Temple.

A few days after, the Dauphin fainted.—Thierry having returned with a surgeon named Soupé, and another called Julapes, this indisposition had no bad consequences.

About this time, Madame Tison went mad. She was uneasy about the Dauphin's illness, and had been long tormented with remorse: she got into a state of languor, and would not take the air. One day she began to talk aloud to herself; and that having made the young princess laugh, her mother and aunt looked at her with an air of satisfaction, as if they observed with pleasure this short moment of gaiety.

But the poor woman's derangement soon became serious: she raved of her crimes, of her denunciations, of prisons, scaffolds, the queen, the royal family, and all their misfortunes. Conscious of her crimes, she believed that the persons against whom she had informed * had perished. Every morning she was in anxious hope of seeing the municipal officers whom she had denounced; and, not seeing them, she went to bed every night in a deeper melancholy. Her dreams must have been dreadful, for she screamed in her sleep so loud, that the princesses heard her.

The municipal officers permitted her to see her daughter, of whom she was very fond.

* See page 60. T.

One day, that the porter, who was not apprized of this permission, had refused to let the daughter come into the prison, the officers, seeing the desperate grief of the mother, sent for the girl at ten o'clock at night. This untimely visit alarmed her still more; it was with great difficulty they persuaded her to go down stairs, and on the way she repeated to her husband "We are going to prison." When she saw her daughter, she did not know her; the fancy of being arrested had seized her mind. She was coming back again with one of the officers, but in the middle of the stairs she suddenly stopped, and would neither go backwards nor forwards. The officer, alarmed, was obliged to call for assistance to remove her up stairs, but nothing could induce her to go to bed, and during the whole night she disturbed the princesses by raving and talking incessantly.

The next morning the physician pronounced her quite mad. She was for ever at the feet of the queen, asking her pardon; and nothing indeed could exceed the compassion which both she and Madame Elizabeth shewed to this poor creature, of whose previous conduct they had had too much reason to complain. They watched and attended her while she remained in this state in the Temple; and they endeavoured to pacify her with the warmest assurances of their forgiveness. The day after, she was removed from the tower to the palace; but her disorder increasing every hour, she was at last sent to the *Hotel Dieu, where a woman belonging to the police was placed to watch her, and to gather whatever she might, in her phrensy, say concerning the royal family.

---

* The general hospital of Paris. T.

On the 3d of July, they read to the princesses a decree of the Convention, that the Dauphin should be separated from them, and placed in the most secure apartment of the tower. As soon as the young prince heard this sentence pronounced, he threw himself into the arms of his mother, and entreated, with violent cries, not to be separated from her. The unhappy queen was stricken to the earth by this cruel order; she would not part with her son, and she actually defended, against the efforts of the officers, the bed in which she had placed him. But these men would have him, and threatened to call up the guard, and use violence. The queen exclaimed, that they had better kill her than tear her child from her. An hour was spent in resistance on her part, in threats and insults from the officers, and in prayers and tears on the part of the two other princesses.

At last they threatened even the life of the child, and the queen's maternal tenderness at length forced her to this sacrifice. Madame Elizabeth and Madame Royale dressed the child, for his poor mother had no longer strength for any thing. Nevertheless, when he was dressed, she took him and delivered him into the hands of the officers, bathing him with her tears, foreseeing possibly that she was never to see him again. The poor little fellow embraced his mother, his aunt, and his sister, and was carried off in tears by the officers. The queen charged them to ask the council-general for permission to see her son, were it only at meals. They engaged to do so. She was overwhelmed with the sorrow of parting with him, but her horror was extreme when she heard that one *Simon, (a shoemaker by trade, whom she had seen in the Temple,) was one of the municipal officers to whom her unhappy child was confided. She asked continually to be allowed to see him, but in vain. He, on his side, cried for two whole days, and asked without intermission for his parents.

The officers no longer remained in the queen's apartment; she and the other two princesses remained locked up together both night and day; but it was an alleviation of their misfortune to be delivered from such society. The guards now came only three

* Simon, a shoemaker, was appointed *guardian* of the Dauphin His chief duty was to debilitate his body and impair his understanding; and he, as we shall see in the text, succeeded but too well in the infernal task. He was involved in Robespierre's overthrow, and was guillotined the day after him, July 29th, 1794. T.

times a day, to bring their meals, and to examine the bolts and bars of the windows.

The princesses had now no one to attend them, and were all the better for it. Madame Elizabeth and the young princess made the beds, and waited on the queen. They often went up to the Tower, because the Dauphin went there: the only pleasure the queen enjoyed was seeing him through a chink as he passed at a distance. She watched at this chink for hours together, to see the child as he passed. She now and then heard of him, either from the officers, or from Tison, who sometimes saw Simon. Tison endeavoured to make compensation for his past conduct; and, to obtain forgiveness for his former cruelties, he told the princesses all he could learn about the Dauphim.

As to Simon, he ill-treated the child beyond

all belief, and the mere so because the poor boy cried at being separated from his family: at last he had overcome him to such a point of dread, that he did not *dare to weep*. Madame Elizabeth, who knew all this, entreated Tison, and those who, through compassion, brought her reports of the state of the Dauphin, to conceal these horrors from the queen; who, however, either knew or suspected them but too well.

One day, a report reached the Convention that the Dauphin had been seen on the Boulevard. The guard at the Temple, no longer seeing him, reported that he was dead; and even the princesses, alas! for a moment *hoped* that this might be true. But all were soon undeceived; the Convention directed him to be taken into the garden, that he might be seen. On this occasion, the young prince, whose faculties they had not yet had time to alienate, complained of being separated from his mother, but they soon obliged him to hold his tongue. As soon as the members of the Convention, who had been sent to ascertain the presence of the Dauphin, had come up to the queen, she made a formal complaint against the cruelty of taking away her child. They answered, that they thought it a necessary precaution.

A new Attorney-General had been lately appointed: he also came to visit the princesses. Notwithstanding all they had been obliged to see and to suffer during their misfortunes, the manners of this man astonished them. From the moment he entered their room till his departure, he did nothing but *swear*.

On the 2d of August, at two o'clock in the morning, they came to awake them, to read to the queen the decree of the Convention, which, on the requisition of the attorney of the Commune, ordered her removal to the *Conciergerie, preparatory to her trial.

The queen heard this decree read without visible emotion, and she did not speak a single word to them. But Madame Elizabeth and Madame Royale immediately required to be allowed to follow the queen: this was refused. During the whole time that the queen was employed in making a bundle of the clothes which she was to take with her, these officers never quitted her. She was even obliged to dress herself before them. They asked for her pockets: she gave them. They searched them, and took away every thing they contained, though there

* The Conciergerie was originally, as the name imports, the *porters' lodge* of the ancient palace of justice, and, as was the case with our *Marshalsea*, became, in process of time, a prison, from the habit of confining there persons who had committed petty offences about the court. T.

was nothing of any importance. They sent them in a parcel to the Revolutionary *Tribunal, and told the queen that this parcel would be opened in her presence, at the tribunal. They left her only a pocket-handkerchief and a smelling-bottle. She was now hurried away, after having embraced her daughter, and charging her to keep up her spirits and courage, to take a tender care

* It may not be uninstructive to give a few details of the tribunal that murdered the queen. It consisted of four judges—Herman, Foucaut, Verteuil, and Lanne—all of whom, except Verteuil, (an apostate priest,) perished on the scaffold within a year. Fouquier-Tinvelle, of bloody memory, was her accuser. This man grew frightened at the success of his prosecutions, and at the numbers he sent to death: he wished to draw back, but it was too late. He was often heard to say "My turn will come." It did come, and he was executed on the 6th of May, 1795. The jury consisted of a wig-maker, a printer, a tailor, a surgeon, a late deputy of the Convention, a crier, a carpenter, a house-painter, &c.; and three at least of these are *known* to have perished on the scaffold within a few months. T.

of her aunt, and to obey her as a second mother: she then threw herself into the arms of her sister, and recommended her children to her care. The young princess was in a kind of trance; and her affliction, at parting with her mother, was so deep and overpowering, that she was unable to speak. At last, Madame Elizabeth having said a few words to the queen, in a whisper, she departed without daring to cast another look on her daughter, lest she should lose her firmness.

She was obliged to stop again at the foot of the tower, because the officers insisted on making a procès-verbal of the delivery of her person. In going out, she struck her forehead against the wicket, not having *stooped

* Mathieu, the goaler, used to say, "I make Madame Veto (the queen), and her sister and daughter, proud as they are, salute me; for the door is so low that they cannot pass without curtseying." T.

low enough. They asked her whether she had not hurt herself: she replied, *No; nothing can hurt me now.* She got into a carriage with one municipal officer and two gendarmes.

On her arrival at the Conciergerie, they put her into the filthiest, dampest, and most unwholesome room of the whole prison. A police soldier guarded her day and night. Madame Elizabeth and Madame Royale spent many days and many nights in tears, though they had assured Madame Elizabeth, when her sister was removed, that no harm should happen to her.

The company of her aunt, whom she tenderly loved, was a great consolation to Madame Royale; but, alas! all that she loved was perishing around her, and she was soon to lose her also.

The day after the queen's removal, Madame Elizabeth entreated with great earnestness to be allowed to join her sister; but she could not obtain this indulgence, nor even any account of her. As she knew that the queen, who never had drunk any thing but water, could not drink that of the Seine, as it did not agree with her, she begged the officers to take her some of that of * Ville D'Avray, which came every day to the Temple. They promised to do so, and made an order accordingly; but one of their colleagues took it into his head to oppose this arrangement, and the order was never carried into effect.

A few days after, the queen, in order to obtain some tidings of her daughter and Madame Elizabeth, endeavoured to send to the

---

* An agreeable little village about half-way between St. Cloud and Versailles. T.

Temple for some things which were useful to her; and, amongst others, her knitting-box, because she had undertaken to knit a pair of stockings for the Dauphin. The princesses sent it to her, and all the silk and worsted they could find, because they knew that the queen was very fond of some kind of work, by way of occupation. They remembered that in happier times she had been very fond of it, and indeed only desisted from it when she was obliged to be in public. All their care, however, was thrown away; and nothing that they had sent was delivered to the queen. They learned afterwards that these things were not delivered. The reason was, an apprehension that she should endeavour to shorten her life, by means of the knitting-needles.

For some time, the two prisoners heard of the Dauphin from the municipal officers.

That, however, did not last; but they heard him every day singing the *Carmagnole*, Marseillais songs, and such trash, with Simon. Simon dressed him in a red hat, and a * carmagnole. He made him sing at the windows, that the guard might hear him; and he taught him the most horrid oaths and execrations against God, his own family, and the aristocrats. The queen fortunately was ignorant of these horrors. She was gone before the child had learned this infamous lesson. It was an infliction which the mercy of Heaven was pleased to spare her.

Before the queen left the Temple, they came to ask her for the Dauphin's clothes. On this occasion, she expressed her wish

---

* I do not know what article of dress they called by this name. I presume it was a kind of jacket. T.

that the son of Louis the Sixteenth should not cease to wear mourning; but the first thing Simon did was to take away his black coat.

Towards the end of August, the change of life, and the ill usage with which he was overwhelmed, made him sick. Simon obliged him to eat to excess, and to drink large quantities of wine, though the child disliked that liquor. This diet soon brought on a fever; for which they gave him physic, which disagreed with him, and his constitution became altogether deranged. He grew extremely fat, without increasing in height or strength. Simon, however, still made him take the air on the leads of the tower.

In the beginning of September, Madame Royale had an indisposition, caused solely by her anxiety about her mother: she never heard a drum that she did not expect another 2d of

September: every day she went upon the leads with her aunt. The officers visited them closely thrice a day, but their severity did not prevent the prisoners receiving now and then some hints of what was passing abroad, and particularly about the queen, which was their greatest concern.

In spite of all the efforts and vigilance of the cruel men about them, the princesses always found some compassionate hearts, whose pity has been useful to them. They heard that the queen was accused of having had a correspondence abroad; they therefore got rid of their writings, their pencils, and whatever they had still preserved, fearing that they might be undressed and searched before Simon's wife, and that finding these things on them might endanger the queen; for they had contrived, notwithstanding the most minute searches which were made in their chambers, and amongst all the furniture, to conceal ink, paper, and pens. They learnt too that the queen might have escaped * from the *Conciergerie*. The wife of the † keeper was not insensible to her misfortunes, and paid her every possible attention.

The officers came again for linen for the queen, but they would not give them any account of her state of health. They took away from the princesses even some pieces of tapestry which they were working, on pre-

* This seems exceedingly doubtful ; there were, I believe, more than one plot for this purpose, but they all seem but little likely to have succeeded. T.

† The keeper's name was Richard. He and his wife both shewed feelings of humanity, which, though in other times they would not have attracted much notice, were, in the then state of France, considered as very extraordinary. T.

tence that these works might contain mysterious characters, and a secret mode of writing.

On the 21st of September, at one in the morning, Hebert arrived with several officers, to execute an order of the Commune, that the two prisoners should be confined more strictly than heretofore; that they should have but one room; that Tison, who did the coarse household work, should be put in prison in the turret; that they should have nothing but what was absolutely necessary; that there should be a kind of slide made in the door of their chamber, by which their victuals were to be conveyed to them; and that, except to bring them water and fire-wood, no person should be allowed to enter the room.

The slide in the door was not made, and the officers still continued to come three times a day, and examine very carefully all the bars and bolts, and every kind of furniture. The princesses made their own beds, and swept the room: this was a long work at first, from their aukwardness at it, but they were obliged to do it, for they had at last absolutely no one to wait upon them. Hebert told Madame Elizabeth that equality was the first law of the French republic; and, other prisoners not being allowed attendants, they could no longer have Tison. In order to treat them with all possible severity, they deprived them of even the most trifling accommodations; an armed chair, for instance, in which Madame Elizabeth used to sit, and several other little matters of the same kind.

When their meals arrived, the doors were suddenly clapped to, that they might not even see the persons who brought them. They no longer heard any news, except by the hawkers, whose cries now and then reached them.

They were forbidden to go on the leads, and were deprived of some large fine sheets, with which they had been indulged, lest, notwithstanding the gratings, they should escape from the windows. This was the pretext alleged; but the real cause of the change was a desire to give them coarse and dirty sheets.

I believe it was about this time that the queen's trial began. I have learnt, since her death, that there was a plan for effecting her escape from the Conciergerie, which unhappily failed. I have been assured that the gendarmes who guarded her, and the wife of the gaoler, had been gained over; that she had seen several well-affected persons in the prison, and, amongst others, a clergyman, who had administered the sacrament to her, which she had received with the utmost devotion.

The opportunity of escaping failed, once, because, instead of speaking to the *second* sentinel, as she had been desired to do, she addressed the *first*. Another time she had already got out of her dungeon, and had passed one of the corridors, when a gendarmes obliged her to turn back, and the whole scheme failed. These attempts will not surprise us if we recollect that all honest men took an interest in the queen's fate, and that, with the exception of the vile and ferocious wretches, who, at that time governed our unhappy country, every one who was permitted to speak to her, see her, or approach her, were touched with pity and respect, so well did her affability temper the dignity of her manners. Madame Elizabeth and Madame Royale knew none of those details while they were passing. They had only heard that a Chevalier de St. Louis had given her a pink with a note concealed in it, but, as they were confined closer than ever, they could not learn the result*.

Every day were the princesses visited and searched by the municipal officers. At four

---

* M. Hue gives the detail of this affair. The Chevalier de Rougeville managed to get invited to dinner at the house of one Michonis, a municipal officer, one of the inspectors of prisons in Paris, and there contrived very adroitly to obtain leave (to gratify his *curiosity*, as he pretended) to see the queen. He wore a nosegay, which he pretended a lady had given him: in this was the pink, which contained a note with these words, "I have men and money at your disposal." When he was admitted to the queen, he offered her the pink. She took it, and found the note; but, as she was endeavouring to trace an answer with the point of a pin, the guard surprised her, and all was discovered. M. de Rougeville escaped, but Michonis, who had no concern in the scheme, was beheaded. T.

o'clock in the morning of the 4th of September, they came to make a complete search, and to carry off every article of plate and china. They took the little that was left; and, as some articles were wanting, they accused the princesses of having stolen them. The princesses of having stolen them!—but it was their colleagues who had been the thieves, and they pretended not to know it. They found, behind a chest of drawers of Madame Elizabeth's, a rouleau of Louis d'ors, which they immediately seized with extraordinary eagerness, and questioned her minutely as to whence it came, how long she had it, and for what use she had kept it. She replied, "That it had been given to her by the Princess de Lamballe after the 10th of August; and that she had preserved it ever since." They then asked her who had given it to Madame de Lamballe. She answered, that she did not know. In fact, Madame de Lamballe's waiting-women had found means to convey this money to her in the Temple; and she had given it to the royal family. They also examined Madame Royale, and asked her her name, as if they had not known it; and made her sign that account of the transaction.

At noon on the 8th of October, while the princesses were employed in dressing themselves, and arranging their bed-room, Pâche, Chaumette, and David*, members of the Con-

* David, a painter, and one of the regicides. When Robespierre was attacked the day before his final overthrow, David addressed him in the enthusiasm of their bloody friendship—"*If you are obliged to drink hemlock, I will drink it with you.*" Next day, however, his appetite for hemlock was gone, and he very prudently took care to let his *Socrates* perish without him. It is said that he saved his life by asking a respite, that he might finish a picture. This is very likely; a false sensibi-

vention, with several officers of the municipality, arrived. Madame Elizabeth, who was not quite dressed, refused to open the door till she was. Pâche, addressing the young princess, begged her to walk down stairs. Her aunt would have followed, but they stopped her. She asked whether her niece would be permitted to come up again; Chaumette assured her that she should. "You may trust," said he, "the word of an honest republican: she shall return."

The young princess embraced Madame Elizabeth, who was greatly affected, and went

---

lity, and a pretence to a taste for the arts, garnished all the *solid* atrocities of the Revolution. David was said to have improved his knowledge of the anatomy of the human figure, by the opportunities which the massacres afforded him. Buonaparte, of course, highly favoured him, and made him a knight of the legion of honour. T.

down * much embarrassed at finding herself for the first time in her life alone with men. She did not know what they wanted with her, but she recommended herself to the protection of God. On the stairs, Chaumette affected to offer her certain civilities: she pretended not to know what he meant, and she ran down into her brother's room, whom she embraced tenderly; but they were soon torn asunder, and the princess was obliged to go into another room. Chaumette desired her to sit down, which she did. He sat down opposite to her, while a municipal officer took out his pen. Chaumette asked her her name, but Hebert continued the interrogatory.

---

* The whole of the following part of the narration proves, if there had been before any doubt, that the relator can be no other than the princess herself. T.

Tell me the truth, he said; it is not intended to affect you or your friends.

Not to affect my mother?

No, but some other persons who have not done their duty. Do you know the Citizens Toulan*, Le Pitre, Breno, Brugnot, Merle, Michonis?

No, sir.

That is false; particularly Toulan, that little young man who used to come so often on duty to the Temple?

I know nothing of him, nor of the rest.

---

* Toulan was really in communication with the queen. He was a violent republican; but the sight of the royal family touched him with pity, and it was said, at the time, a tenderer sentiment. It would seem, from Hebert's questions, that he partook this latter opinion, though it now appears that Madame Royale did not know Toulan. He was guillotined in June, 1794. T.

Do you remember that you were one day alone with your brother in the turret?

Yes.

Your parents had sent you thither, that they might be more at their ease to speak to these people?

No, sir, but to accustom us to cold.

What did you do in the turret?

We talked and played with one another.

When you came out, did you not observe what these men had brought to your parents?

I did not see any thing.

Chaumette then questioned her about a thousand shocking things, of which they accused her mother and her aunt. She was so struck at hearing such horrors, and so indignant at these questions, that, terrified as she was, she could not help exclaiming, that they were infamous falsehoods; but, although she began to weep, Hebert only insisted the more violently.

He put several questions to her, which she did not comprehend, but of which she understood enough to make her cry with indignation and horror.

He then asked her several questions about Varennes and other things, to all which she answered as well as she could, without implicating any body. She had always heard her parents say, that it were better to die than implicate any body.

At last, about three o'clock, the examination was finished; it had lasted from noon. She entreated Chaumette to let her rejoin her mother, saying, with truth, that she had often made the same request of her aunt. "It is out of my power," said he. "*What, Sir, you could not obtain this favour from the general council?*" "No, I have no authority there." He then sent her back to her apartment with the municipal officers, desiring her not to speak of what had passed to her aunt, whom they were going to examine. When she reached her room, she threw herself into the arms of her aunt; but they were soon separated, and the latter taken down stairs.

They put the same questions to her as they had done to Madame Royale, relative to the men before mentioned. She answered, that she knew the persons and names of these officers and others, but that she had no kind of intercourse with them. She denied having any correspondence without the Temple, and she replied with still more contempt to the shocking things about which they examined her also.

She returned at four o'clock: her examination lasted but an hour, because the deputies saw that they had no chance of intimidating her as they had hoped to be able to do a young person by the length and grossness of their inquiries. They were, however, much deceived: they forgot that the life which Madame Royale had lived for four years past, and, above all, the example of courage shewn her by the parents, had given her a degree of energy and strength of mind far beyond her years.

Chaumette had assured the princesses that this interrogatory had no concern with the queen, and that they were not thinking of trying her. Alas! he deceived them: she was immediately after put upon her trial, and condemned to death; but the princesses were not aware of it. The following are the only particulars which they afterwards heard of this infamous trial. First, the names of her two counsel*; and that Mathieu and Simon, gaolers of the Temple, were examined, as well as several worthy persons, whom the queen was sorry to see involved on her account. They learnt also that the doctor, Brunier, had been brought before the court. They asked him if he knew the queen. " *Yes.*" " How long?" " *Since* 1788, *when the queen intrusted to me the care of her children's health.*" " When you went to the Temple, you facilitated the prisoners' correspondence with persons without the walls?" The queen then said, " *Doctor Brunier, as you all know, never came to the*

---

* M. Tronçon-Ducoudray and Chaveau Lagarde. The former was exiled to Cayenne, where he died in 1798. The latter is still alive, and has received the thanks and favour of the royal family, and particularly of Madame D'Angoulême. They both shewed great talents and courage. T.

Temple but in company with a municipal officer, and never spoke to us but in his presence." And, finally, they heard, that the trial had lasted three days and nights without intermission. They put the most unworthy, the most horrid, questions to her. Every body knows the noble answer she made to one of the most shocking. The people were touched at it, and her judges precipitated the sentence, from a dread of the effect which her dignity, presence of mind, and innocence, might have upon the people. She listened to it with perfect composure. They sent to attend her, in her last moments, a priest who had taken the new constitutional oaths. She at first declined his assistance with gentleness, and afterwards positively refused to listen to him or accept his ministry. She knelt down, and prayed alone for a considerable time, coughed a little, then went to bed, and slept for some hours. Next morning, learning that the rector of St. Margaret's was in a part of the prison opposite to her's, she knelt down at the window facing his. It is said that this clergyman perceived her, and gave her absolution, or his benediction. Then, having thus offered her life as a sacrifice to her Maker, she went to death with fortitude, amidst the execrations which a misguided multitude were uttering against her. Her courage did not abandon her in the cart or on the scaffold; and she shewed it at her death, as she had done during her life.

Thus died, on the 16th of October, 1793, Marie-Antoinette-Josephe-Jeanne de Lorraine, daughter of an emperor, and wife of a king. She was thirty-seven years and eleven months old. She had been twenty-three years in France, and had survived her husband eight months.

The princesses could not persuade themselves that the queen was dead, though they heard her sentence cried about by the newsmen. A hope, natural to the unfortunate, made them believe that she had been saved.

There were moments, however, at which, in spite of their reliance on foreign powers, they felt the liveliest alarm for her, when they heard the fury of the unhappy populace against the whole family. Madame Royale remained for eighteen months in this cruel suspense.

The princesses learnt, by the cries of the newsmen, the death of the duke of Orleans; it was the only piece of news that reached them during the whole winter. It gave them a ray of hope; but the searches were soon renewed, and they were treated with increased rigour. Madame Elizabeth, who had had since the Revolution an issue in her arm, found the greatest difficulty in procuring the necessary dressings for it: they were for a long while absolutely prohibited; but at last one of the municipal officers remonstrated on the cruelty of such conduct, and procured her the proper ointment. They also prevented her making a kind of herb-tea, which Madame Royale took every morning, on account of her health. Being no longer allowed fish on fast-days, they asked for eggs, or something else, which they could eat, without violating their religious scruples. They were refused, on the ground that equality admitted of no difference of days, that weeks had been abolished, that decades had been substituted in their room, and that Fridays and Sundays no longer existed; and they gave them an almanac of this new fashion.

One fast-day, that Madame Royale asked for something to eat, consistent with her religious opinions, they said to her, "*But Citizen, do you not know what is going on in the world? None but fools believe in that stuff now-a-days.*" She never made a second request.

They still continued their visits of search, particularly in the month of November, when the prisoners were ordered to be searched three times a day. One of their searches lasted from four o'clock in the evening to half past eight. The officers who made it were quite intoxicated. It is impossible to give any idea of their language, their insults, their curses, during these four hours. They carried away even the most trifling articles, such as hats, court cards, because they are called kings and queens, and books which happened to have coats of arms in them. They, however, left the princesses their religious books, after ridiculing them in every term of filth and blasphemy which they could devise.

Simon accused the princesses of forging assignats, and of having corresponded with the king during his trial; these charges he made in the name of the poor little Dauphin, whom he forced to sign these falsehoods. Madame Elizabeth had taught her niece the game of tric-trac to divert her, and the noise they made in playing was represented by Simon as coining; they, however, played tric-trac during the winter, which, in spite of the visits and searches of their inquisitors, passed away quietly enough. They gave them fire-wood, which they had at first refused them.

[1794.]—On the 19th of January, they heard a great noise in the Dauphin's apartment, and they guessed he was going to be removed from the Temple: they were convinced of this, when, looking through the key-hole, they saw several parcels carried away. On the subsequent days they heard the doors open, and the sound of footsteps in the room; satisfied, therefore, that the Dauphin was gone, they believed that some person of importance had been placed in his apartment. It was Simon who was gone: obliged to choose between the situations of municipal officer and guardian of the Dauphin, he had preferred the former, and they had had the cruelty to leave the poor child absolutely alone. Unheard-of and unexampled barbarity! to leave an unhappy and sickly infant, of eight years old, in a great room, locked and bolted in, with no other resource than a broken bell, which he never rang, so greatly did he dread the people whom its sound would have brought to him; he preferred wanting any thing, and every thing, to calling for his persecutors. His bed had not been stirred for six months, and he had not strength to make it himself—it was alive with bugs, and vermin still more disgusting. His linen and his person were covered with them. For more than a year he had had no change of shirt or stockings; every kind of filth was allowed to accumulate about him, and in his room; and, during all that period, nothing of that kind had been removed. His window, which was locked as well as grated, was never opened; and the infectious smell of this horrid room was so dreadful, that no one could bear it for a moment. He might, indeed, have washed himself, for he had a pitcher of water, and have kept himself somewhat more clean than he did; but, overwhelmed by the ill treatment he had received, he had not resolution to do so, and his illness began to deprive him of even the necessary strength. He never asked for any thing, so great was his dread of Simon and his other keepers. He passed his days without any kind of occupation. They did not even allow him light in the evening. This situation affected his mind as well as his body, and it is not surprising that he should have fallen into a frightful atrophy. The length of time which he resisted this persecution proves how good his constitution must have originally been.

Madame Elizabeth kept Lent strictly. She dined on a cup of milk-coffee, which she saved from her breakfast, and, for supper, ate only dry bread. She, however, made Madame Royale eat what was given her, because her youth did not require nor permit that she should fast; but, as for herself, nothing could be more exemplary than her way of life. Though they had done all they could to deprive her of the means of obeying the dictates of her conscience in these particulars, she had not, on that account, neglected any of the duties of religion.

In the beginning of spring they were refused candles, and they were obliged to go to bed as soon as it grew dark.

Until the 9th of May nothing extraordinary happened. On that day, at the moment they were going to bed, the outside bolts of the doors were drawn, and a knocking was heard. Madame Elizabeth begged of them to wait till she had put on her gown; but they answered that they could not wait, and knocked so violently, that they were near bursting open the door. When she was dressed, she opened the door, and they immediately said to her, "Citizen, come down."—"*And my niece?*"—"We shall take care of her afterwards." She embraced her niece; and, in order to calm her agitation, promised to return. "No, citizen," said they, "you shall not return;—take your bonnet, and come along." They overwhelmed her with the grossest abuse. She bore it all patiently, and embraced her niece again, exhorting her to have confidence in Heaven, to follow the principles of religion in which she had been educated, and never to forget the last commands of her father and mother. She then left her.

Down stairs they detained her a considerable time in searching her, (though they found nothing,) and in writing an account of their proceedings. At length, after a thousand insults, she was put into a hackney-coach, with the crier of the revolutionary court, and taken to the Conciergerie, where she passed the night. The next morning they asked her these questions:—

What is your name?

Elizabeth, of France.

Where were you on the 10th of August?

In the palace of the Thuilleries, with my brother.

What have you done with your jewels?

I know nothing about them; besides, these questions are wholly useless. You are determined on my death. I have offered to Heaven the sacrifice of my life; and I am ready to die, happy at the prospect of rejoining in a better world those whom I loved upon earth!

They condemned her to death. She asked to be placed in the same room with the other persons who were to die with her. She exhorted them, with a presence of mind, an elevation of soul, and religious enthusiasm, which fortified all their minds. In the cart she preserved the same firmness, and encouraged and supported the women who accompanied her. At the scaffold they had the barbarity to reserve her for the last. All the women, in leaving the cart, begged to embrace her. She kissed them, and, with her usual benignity, said some words of comfort to each. Her strength never abandoned her, and she died with all the resignation of the purest piety. Her soul was separated from her body, and ascended to receive its reward from the merciful Being, whose worthy servant she had been.

Marie Phillipine Elizabeth-Helene, sister of Louis XVI., died on the 10th May, 1794, at the age of thirty years. She had been, during all her life, a model of virtue. From the age of fifteen, she had dedicated herself to piety, and the means of her salvation. Since 1790, when I was in a situation to appreciate her merits, I saw in her nothing but the love of God and the horror of sin, religion, gentleness, meekness, modesty, and a devoted attachment to her family; she sacrificed her life for them, for nothing could persuade her to leave the king and queen. She was, in short, a princess worthy of the blood to which she belonged*.

It is impossible to imagine the desolation of Madame Royale when she found herself separated from her revered companion. She did not know what had become of her, and could

* It is said that Madame Royale resembled her in feature: it is certain that the young Princess, after receiving from her aunt the care and councils of a mother, inherited her character and her virtues.

not learn. She passed several nights in great anxiety, but, though very uneasy, she was far from believing that her aunt's death was so near. When she considered the manner in which she had been carried off, she could not but entertain the greatest fears for her; yet she tried to persuade herself that they would only banish her from France.

Next day she inquired what had become of her aunt. The officers replied, "that she was gone to take the air." She said, "that since she was to be separated from her aunt, she hoped she would be allowed to rejoin her mother." They said they would speak about it. They then brought her the key of a press, in which Madame Elizabeth had kept her linen. She wished to send her some, as she had gone without any. They answered, that they could not permit it. To all her entreaties to see her mother, or hear of her aunt, these men always answered, that they would speak about it.

At last, seeing that all these endeavours were fruitless, and recollecting that her aunt had told her, if ever she should be left alone, to ask for a female attendant, she did so in obedience to her advice; but she did so reluctantly, for she was sure of being refused, or of having a woman as wicked as those who sent her. In fact, the municipal officers answered this request by telling her that she did not want a woman, and by redoubling their rigour towards her. They even took away her knife which had been before returned to her. They obliged her to undergo an examination about a tinder-box, of which they wanted to deprive her. Similar scenes were renewed every day, but the princess only answered when they put direct questions to her.

The Dauphin still remained in solitude and filth. His keepers never went near him but to give him his meals. They had no compassion for this unhappy child. There was one of the guards, whose gentle manners encouraged the princess to recommend her brother to his attention: this man ventured to complain of the severity with which the boy was treated, but he was dismissed next day.

For herself, she asked nothing but what was indispensable, and even this was often harshly refused; but she, at least, could keep herself clean. She had soap and water, and carefully swept out her room every day. She had no light; but in the long days she did not feel much this privation. They would not give her any more books; but she had some religious works and some travels, which she had read over and over. She also had her knitting, which tired her very much *.

The 9th † Thermidor arrived; Madame Royale heard the drums beating to arms, the tocsin ringing, and was very uneasy. The officers who were in the Temple never stirred out. When her dinner was brought, she was afraid to ask what the matter was; but on the 10th Thermidor, at six o'clock in the morning, she heard a frightful noise in the Temple. The

* There is a singular naiveté in the original expression; "Elle avait aussi un tricot *qui l'ennuyait beaucoup*." It describes admirably the irksomeness of this solitary and worn-out amusement, which, though it tired her, she could not help continuing. T.

† 27th of July, 1794, the day of the overthrow of Robespierre. T.

guards were calling to arms, the drums were rolling, and doors opening and shutting with violence. All this tumult was, it seems, occasioned by a visit of some members of the National Assembly (the Convention), who came to see that all was quiet. She heard the doors of her brother's room open; she then got up, and was already dressed by the time the deputies came to her room. There were Barras*, and several others: they were in their official full dress, which surprised the princess, who was not accustomed to see them so fine. Barras called her by her name, and was surprised to

* Barras, of a noble family of Provence, a conventionalist, a regicide, and at last a director. He was Buonaparte's first patron; and, when the latter attained the supreme power, became, as is natural with such worthies, his first victim. He amassed enormous wealth, and settled himself, after Buonaparte's ingratitude, in his native province, where he lived in the enjoyment of his ill-gotten riches, till the law for banishing the regicides disturbed his luxurious retirement. T.

find her up. They soon went away; and she heard them haranguing the guards under the windows, and exhorting them to be faithful to the National Convention. There were great shouts of *Vive la Republique! Vive la Convention!* The guard was doubled, and the three municipal officers, who were in the Temple, remained there eight days. In the evening of the third day, about half past nine, as she was lying in bed, because she had no light, but not able to sleep from anxiety as to what was going on, they knocked at her door, to introduce her to Laurent, the commissioner appointed by the Convention for the custody of herself and her brother.

Next morning, at ten o'clock, Laurent* came into her room, and inquired politely

---

* I am sorry not to be able to give any account of Laurent. T.

whether she wanted any thing. He always visited her three times a day, but behaved with civility, and, in addressing her, he did not *thee*-and-*thou* (*tutoyer*) her. He never searched the drawers, nor other pieces of furniture.

At the end of three days, the Convention sent a deputation to ascertain the situation of the Dauphin. The members were struck with pity at the state in which they found him, and directed that he should be better treated. Laurent got him a clean bed, the old one being filled with bugs and vermin: he made him bathe himself, and cleansed him from the filth with which he was covered. However, they still left him alone.

The princess asked Laurent after her mother and aunt, of whose deaths she was still ignorant. He replied, with an air of concern, that her inquiries should not be addressed to him.

Next day came some men in *scarfs, to whom she repeated the same question, and they gave the same answer. They added, that they did not see why she should wish to be released, as she seemed to be very comfortable. "*It is dreadful,*" she replied, "*to be separated for more than a year from one's mother, without even hearing what is become of her, or of her sister.*" "You are not ill?"

* One of the fopperies of the Revolution was the costumes and scarfs which the public functionaries, as they were called, wore. This absurdity is not yet quite disused; the members of the Chambers of Peers and Deputies have still a peculiar costume. It is not unusual to see some of these gentlemen in a fine embroidered coat, over their other ordinary clothes, and wearing perhaps the dirty boots in which they walked to the assembly. They should be *either* in full costume, or in their usual dress: the mixture is ridiculous. T.

"*No, Sir, but the cruellest illness is that of the heart.*" "I tell you again, that we can do nothing for you; but I advise you to be patient, and submit to the justice and goodness of the French people."

She was exposed*, by the explosion which took place at the plain of Grenelle, to great alarm.

During all this time, the Dauphin still remained alone. Laurent visited him thrice a day, but he was afraid to shew him all the attention he wished, for he was closely watched. He took, however, more care of Madame Royale, who had every reason to be satisfied with him during the whole time of his attendance. He frequently inquired whether

* The original passage is somewhat obscurely expressed, but its meaning is obvious. T.

she wanted any thing, and begged her to ask for what she might wish for, and to ring her bell when she wanted any thing. He gave her back her tinder-box, and allowed her candles.

In the beginning of November, certain civil commissioners came. They were men chosen, one from each section, to pass twenty-four hours in the Temple, to ascertain the existence of the Dauphin. Another commissioner also, called *Gomier, came to assist Laurent. He took extraordinary care of the young king. For a great while, this child had had no light. Gomier obtained leave to give him a candle at night-fall; he even used

* M. Hue calls him Gomin, and another account Gomain. He accompanied Madame to the frontier, when she was exchanged for the deputies who had been delivered to the Austrians by Dumouriez. T.

to pass several hours with him, to amuse him. Gomier soon saw that his wrists and knees were swelled; he was afraid the joints were about to grow callous. He mentioned it to the committee, and asked permission to take him to exercise in the garden. At first, he only removed him to the little parlour, which delighted the child, who was fond of a change of place. He soon felt the attentions of Gomier, and became fond of him: the poor boy had been long unaccustomed to kindness. There is no example of such studied barbarity to a child.

On the 19th of December, the Committee of Public Safety came to the Temple, in consequence of his illness. The members also visited Madame Royale, but did not speak to her.

[1795.]—The winter passed quietly enough;

the keepers were civil, and even lighted the princess's fire for her; they allowed her as much fire-wood as she wanted, which pleased her greatly. They also gave her such books as she wished for. Laurent had already procured her several. Her greatest misfortune now was, that she could hear no tidings of her mother and aunt.

During the winter, the Dauphin had some attacks of fever. He could not be kept away from the fire. Laurent and Gomier used to coax him up to the leads to take the air, but he was hardly there when he complained of not being able to walk, and wished to go down again: he grew worse, and his knees swelled greatly.

Laurent was now removed; but a worthy man of the name of Loine took his place, and, with Gomier, attended the child. In the beginning of spring they persuaded Madame Royale to go up to the leads, which she did. The illness of her brother grew worse every day; his strength diminished; his mind even was affected by the severity he had suffered so long.

The Committee of Public Safety sent Dessault, a surgeon, to attend him: he promised to cure him, though he admitted the disease was very dangerous. Dessault died, and Messrs. Dumangin and Pelletan were appointed to succeed him. They had from the beginning no hope; they gave him, however, some medicines, which he swallowed with great difficulty. He fortunately did not suffer much. It was rather a wasting away than positive pain. He had several alarming crises. The fever increased, his strength diminished, and he expired without pain.

Thus died, on the 9th of June, 1795, at three o'clock in the afternoon, Louis XVII., ten years and two months old. Even his keepers wept for him, so much had his amiable qualities endeared him to them. He had had great talents. He was not poisoned, as some have believed. The only poison that shortened his days was filth, made more fatal by horrible treatment, by harshness and cruelty, of which there is no example*.

---

* Here end *our (sic in orig.)* Memoirs. Madame Royale remained in the Temple six months after the death of her brother, and left it on the 19th of December, 1795, the seventeenth anniversary of her birth. M. Hue, in his work, relates what passed on this occasion, and whatever information he could collect relative to the last months of the princess's confinement.

POSTSCRIPT.

M. de Malesherbes has left a Journal, containing the following Details upon what passed in the Temple, between Louis XVI. and himself.

THE moment I received permission to enter the apartment of the king, I hastened thither. On perceiving me, he immediately quitted a Tacitus, which lay open before him on a small table. He embraced me, his eyes filled with tears, and he said to me, "Your sacrifice is so much the more generous, that you will expose your own life, and you will not save mine." I observed to him that there was no danger for me; that, besides, I at once fulfilled the most sacred of duties, and the warmest wishes of my heart; and that I hoped we might save him by a successful defence. He replied, " I am certain that they will put me to death; they have both the power and the will; nevertheless, let us attend to my trial as if I were likely to succeed; and indeed I shall succeed, for my memory shall be without a stain. But when will the two counsel come?" He had seen Tronchet in the Constituent Assembly, but was not acquainted with Desèze. He made some inquiries concerning the latter, and appeared much satisfied with the account I gave of him.

He was every day employed with us in analyzing the various documents, suggesting arguments, and refuting charges, with a presence of mind and firmness which filled his other advocates as well as myself with admiration, and of which they availed themselves by taking notes in addition to their own. We flattered ourselves that we might hope for a sentence of banishment. We mentioned this to him; and by our reasonings in support of this idea we alleviated the acuteness of his feelings. He entertained the idea for some days; but the public papers undeceived him, and proved that we must abandon any such hope.

When Desèze had drawn up his speech, he read it to us. I have never heard any thing more pathetic than the conclusion; it drew tears from us; but the king said to him—"*It must be omitted; I do not wish to touch their feelings.*"

On another occasion, when we were alone, he said to me—"One thing distresses me much: Desèze and Tronchet owe me nothing; they devote to me their time, their talents, and perhaps their lives; what return can I make for such services? I have nothing left: if I made a bequest in their favour, it would not be carried into effect: but, indeed, it is not with money that such a debt can be discharged." "Sire," I replied, "their own conscience and posterity will confer on them their just reward. But you may yourself bestow one which will overpay them." "*How?*" "Embrace them, sire." The following day the king folded them in his arms, and they shed tears whilst they seized his hands.

The day of trial was approaching, when he, one morning, said to me, "My sister has mentioned to me a worthy clergyman, who has not taken the oath, and whose obscure station may hereafter shelter him from persecution: this is his direction. Will you go to him, speak with him, and prepare him to come, when I shall have obtained permission to see him?" He added, "This is a strange commission for a * *philosopher*, as I know you to be; but, if you had suffered as much as I have, and were about to die, as I am, I should wish you to enjoy those religious sentiments, which would support and console you much better than philosophy. My dear Monsieur de Malesherbes, it is with all my heart that I pray to God to enlighten you."

After the sitting, at which he and his ad-

---

* *Philosophe* and infidel were synonymous terms, since Voltaire had persuaded the wits of Paris that religion was a superstition, and that, to deny Christ, was the test of good sense. T.

vocates had been heard at the Bar, he said to me, "You now perceive that, from the first instant, I was not mistaken, and that my sentence was pronounced before I had been heard." On my return from the Assembly, where we had urged an appeal to the people, and where we had all three spoken, I told him, that, on coming out, I had been surrounded by a great number of persons, who had assured me that he should not perish, or, at least, not till *after* they themselves, and their friends, had died in the attempt to save him. He said to me, "Do you know them? Return to the Assembly instantly; try to find them: tell them that I should never forgive them if a drop of blood were shed on my account. I would not consent that any should be spilled, when, perhaps, it might have saved my throne and my life;

and I do not repent my forbearance." I was the first who announced his sentence to him: his back was turned to a lamp which stood on the chimney, his elbows on the table, and his face covered with his hands. The noise I made in entering roused him from his meditation: he looked steadily at me, and, rising, said to me, "For two days I have been occupied in considering, whether, during the course of my reign, I have deserved the slightest reproach from my subjects: well, M. de Malesherbes, I declare to you, with all the sincerity of my heart, as a man about to appear before his God, that I have always wished and laboured for the happiness of my people; and I have not, in my whole life, had one idea, that was inconsistent with this feeling of my heart." I saw, once more, my unfortunate sovereign: two municipal officers were standing by his side: he also stood, and was reading. One of them told me to speak to him, adding, that they should not listen. I assured the king that the priest he had wished for was coming: he embraced me, and said, "Death does not alarm me: I have the greatest confidence in the mercy of God."

THE END.

Printed by W. CLOWES,
Northumberland-court, Strand, London.

Albemarle-street, London,
February, 1817.

WORKS IN THE PRESS.

JOURNAL of the late CAPTAIN TUCKEY, on a Voyage of Discovery in the Interior of Africa, to explore the Source of the Zaire, or Congo; with a Survey of that River beyond the Cataracts, *published by* AUTHORITY: one volume 4to. uniformly with Park and Adams's Travels.

*** The Journals of this lamented Commander have been received complete, to the farthest point to which he proceeded in the Interior of Southern Africa; and with the Journals and Papers of the Naturalists, &c., who accompanied the Expedition, will be sent to the press as soon after the arrival of the Collections of Natural History, &c., now on board H. M. S. Congo, as they can be properly arranged. With an Introduction, explanatory of the grounds on which the Expedition was undertaken, and of other matters connected with it.

An AUTHENTIC NARRATIVE of the Loss of the AMERICAN BRIG COMMERCE, wrecked on the Western Coast of Africa, in the Month of August, 1815; with an Account of the Sufferings of her surviving Officers and Crew, who were enslaved by the wandering Arabs on the Great African Desert, or Zahahrah; and Observations, historical, geographical, &c., made during the Travels of the Author, while a Slave to the Arabs, and in the Empire of Morocco. By JAMES RILEY, late Master and Supercargo. Preceded by a brief Sketch of the Author's Life; and concluded by a Description of the famous City of Tombuctoo, on the River Niger, and of another large city, far south of it, on the same river, called Wassanah; narrated to the Author at Mogadore, by Side Hamet, an Arabian Merchant; with a portrait of the Author, and a map. Printed in 4to. uniformly with PARK'S, ADAMS'S, and TUCKEY'S TRAVELS.

The PLAYS and POEMS of JAMES SHIRLEY, now first collected and chronologically arranged, and the Text carefully collated and restored. With occasional Notes, and a Biographical and Critical Essay. By WILLIAM GIFFORD, Esq. Handsomely printed by Bulmer, in 6 vol. 8vo. uniformly with MASSINGER and BEN JONSON.

LAOU-SENG-URH; or, "AN HEIR in his OLD AGE;" a Chinese Comedy; being the second Drama ever translated from the original Chinese into any language. By J. F. DAVIS, Esq. of Canton: with a short introductory Essay on the Chinese Drama, small 8vo.

*** This Drama was selected for translation out of the same collection of one hundred ancient plays from which Père Premare translated the "*Orphan of Tchao*," afterwards adapted for the French Stage by Voltaire, and for the English by Murphy.

SPECIMENS of the BRITISH POETS, with Biographical and Critical Notices, and an introductory Essay on British Poetry. By THOMAS CAMPBELL, Esq. Author of the Pleasures of Hope, &c. in 4 vols. post 8vo.

THE UNEDITED ANTIQUITIES OF ATTICA, comprising the Architectural Remains of ELEUSIS, RHAMNUS, SUNIUM, and THORICUS.

*** Published by the Dilettanti Society, handsomely printed in Imperial Folio, with eighty-four Engravings, price 10*l*. 10*s*. in boards.

OUTLINES of GEOLOGY. Being the Substance of a Course of Lectures delivered in the Royal Institution of Great Britain, by W. T. BRANDE, Sec. R. S. F.R.S.E. Prof. Chem. R. I. 8vo.

JOURNEY through ASIA MINOR, ARMENIA, and KOORDISTAN, in the years 1813 and 1814. With Remarks on the Marches of Alexander, and the Retreat of the Ten Thousand. By JOHN MACDONALD KENNEIR, 4to.

ALGEBRA of the HINDUS, with Arithmetic and Mensuration; translated from the Sanscrit. By H. T. COLEBROOKE, Esq. 4to.

The FOURTH and concluding Volume of CAPTAIN BURNEY'S History of Voyages and Discoveries in the South Seas. With a copious Index, 4to.

This work comprises all the Voyages and Discoveries antecedent to the reign of his present Majesty, bringing down their History until the point where Hawkesworth's Collection begins.

Boooks lately published.

ON THE SUPPLY OF EMPLOYMENT AND SUBSISTENCE for the Labouring Classes, in Fisheries, Manufactures, and the Cultivation of Waste Lands; with Remarks on the Operation of the Salt Duties, and a Proposal for their Repeal. By Sir THOMAS BERNARD, Bart. 8vo. 3*s.*

ON THE APPLICATION OF PUBLIC SUBSCRIPTIONS, in providing Employment and Relief for the Labouring Classes. By a Member of the University of Oxford, 8vo. 1*s.* 6*d.*

STATEMENTS RESPECTING THE EAST-INDIA COLLEGE, with an Appeal to Facts; in Refutation of the Charges lately brought against it. By the Rev. T. R. MALTHUS, 8vo. 3*s.* 6*d.*

A Fifth Volume, in small 8vo. of LORD BYRON'S WORKS, containing the Siege of Corinth, Parisina, Fare Thee Well, Monody on Sheridan, and several other Poems, fc. 8vo. 7*s.* 6*d.*

The GUARDIANS; or, FARO-TABLE: a Comedy, as performed at Drury-Lane Theatre. By the late JOHN TOBIN, Esq. Author of the Honey-Moon, 8vo. 3*s.*

The LIFE of RAFFAELLO of URBINO. By the Author of the Life of Michael Angelo, in 8vo. 8*s.* 6*d.*

STORIES selected from the **HISTORY** of ENGLAND. For Children. SECOND EDITION. Bound, 3*s*.

"I was led (says the Author in his Preface) to tell my little girl the following stories, which I found to amuse her in a very high degree, without having any of the disadvantages which result from relations merely fictitious. My principal object was not to *instruct* but to *amuse*, and I therefore did not attempt any thing like a course of history; but, as I have, in general, adhered to historical fact, and departed from it only (when History was doubtful or silent) in favour of some popular prejudices, whatever lasting impression may be made on the young mind will be, on the whole, consistent with truth, and conducive to its further and more substantial improvement. As these stories have appeared to answer my purpose in the individual case, I think it right to offer them to the Public, and shall be glad to hear that they are as successful in other families as they have been in my own."

AN ACCOUNT of the singular Habits and Circumstances of the PEOPLE of the TONGA ISLANDS, in the South Pacific Ocean. By Mr. WILLIAM MARINER, of the PORT AU PRINCE, private Ship of War, the greater part of whose crew was massacred by the natives of Lefooga; 2 vols. 8vo. with a Portrait, 24*s*.

TALES OF MY LANDLORD. THIRD Edition. In four Volumes, 12mo. 28*s*.

ARMATA: a FRAGMENT. 8vo. 8*s*. 6*d*.

NARRATIVE of a **RESIDENCE** in **BELGIUM** during the Campaign of 1815, and of a Visit to the FIELD of WATERLOO, by an ENGLISHWOMAN. 8vo. 10*s*. 6*d*.

CURIOSITIES of **LITERATURE**. Sixth Edition, (with an additional Volume,) 3 vols. 8vo. 36*s*.

The THIRD Volume is sold separately, 12*s*.

THE COMFORTS of OLD AGE. With Biographical Illustrations. By Sir THOMAS BERNARD, Bart. Second Edition, small 8vo. 8*s*. 6*d*.

JOURNAL of a TOUR in GERMANY, SWEDEN, RUSSIA, POLAND, &c. during the Years 1813 and 1814. By J. T. JAMES, Esq. Student of Christ-Church, Oxford. A new Edition, in 2 volumes, 8vo. with Plates, 24*s*.

TRAVELS in the INTERIOR of AFRICA of ROBERT ADAMS, who was detained three years in Slavery by the Arabs of the Great Desert, and resided several Months at Tombuctoo. With a Map. Printed uniformly with Park's Travels, in 4to. 25*s*.

TRAVELS in the INTERIOR DISTRICTS of AFRICA; performed in the years 1795-6-7, and during a subsequent Mission in 1805. By MUNGO PARK. To which is prefixed a copious Life of Mr. PARK. A new Edition, in 2 volumes, 8vo. price 1*l*. 4*s*.

*** The Second Volume contains Mr. PARK'S LAST JOURNEY and LIFE, and may be had separately, price 12*s*.

TRAVELS ABOVE the CATARACTS of EGYPT. By THOMAS LEGH, Esq. M. P. with a Map, 4to. 21*s*.

THE EAST-INDIA GAZETTEER, containing particular Descriptions of the Countries comprehended under the general name of the EAST INDIES, with an Account of the Manners, Customs, Institutions, Manufactures, Commerce, Castes, Religion, &c. of their various Inhabitants. By WALTER HAMILTON, Esq. Handsomely printed in one large volume, 8vo. 25*s*.